D1710265

TECHNOLOGY IN ANCIENT CULTURES

ANCIENT

MEDICAL

TECHNOLOGY

FROM HERBS TO SCALPELS

Michael Woods and
Mary B. Woods

TF
CB

Twenty—First Century Books · Minneapolis

To John and Margaret Woods Starr,
and Cathleen Woods and David Powders

Twenty-First Century Books
A division of Lerner Publishing Group, Inc.
241 First Avenue North
Minneapolis, MN 55401 U.S.A.

Website address: www.lernerbooks.com

Library of Congress Cataloging-in-Publication Data

Woods, Michael, 1946–
    Ancient medical technology : from herbs to scalpels / by Michael Woods and Mary B. Woods.
        p.   cm. – (Technology in ancient cultures)
    Includes bibliographical references and index.
    ISBN 978-0-7613-6522-8 (lib. bdg. : alk. paper)
    1. Medicine, Ancient—Juvenile literature. 2. Materia medica, Vegetable—History—Juvenile literature.
    3. Medical innovations—History—Juvenile literature. I. Woods, Mary B. (Mary Boyle), 1946– II. Title.
    R135.W734 2011
    610.938—dc22   2010028445
Manufactured in the United States of America
1 – PC – 12/31/10

TABLE OF CONTENTS

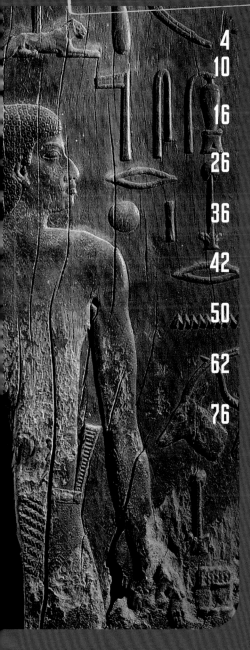

IRELAND

EUROPE

ANCIENT
GREECE

Euphrates R.
Tigris R.

ASIA

ANCIENT
CHINA

Tiber R.

Rome
Athens

Constantinople

Pompeii

Pergamum

Yellow
R.

KOS

Mediterranean Sea

MESOPOTAMIA
(Ancient Middle East)

Indus
R.

ANCIENT
INDIA

ROMAN
EMPIRE

Alexandria

ANCIENT
EGYPT

ARABIAN
PENINSULA

SRI
LANKA

AFRICA

INDIAN OCEAN

ATLANTIC
OCEAN

AUSTRALIA

INTRODUCTION

What do you think of when you hear the word *technology*? You probably think of something totally new. You might think of research laboratories filled with computers, powerful microscopes, and other scientific tools. But technology doesn't refer to just brand-new machines and discoveries. Technology is as old as humankind.

Technology is the use of knowledge and inventions to make human life better. The word *technology* comes from two Greek words. One, *tekhne*, means "art" or "craft." The other, *logos*, means "word" or "speech." The ancient Greeks used *technology* to mean a discussion of arts and crafts. In modern times, the word usually refers to a craft, a technique, or a tool itself.

▲ This marble carving from Oropus, Greece, shows a doctor treating a patient's shoulder. The carving dates from 400 to 350 B.C. In modern times, the carving is housed at the National Archaeological Museum in Athens, Greece.

People use many kinds of technology. Farming is one kind of technology. Transportation and construction are also kinds of technologies. These technologies and many others help make human life easier, safer, and more enjoyable. This book looks at another important kind of technology—one that has helped human life tremendously. That technology is medicine.

A MATTER OF LIFE AND DEATH
People in most ancient societies lived close to nature. To get meat, they didn't go to the supermarket. They killed animals, skinned them, and prepared the meat themselves. When a woman was ready to have a baby, she didn't go to the hospital. She had the baby at home. Female family members assisted in the birth.

Ancient peoples were very familiar with sickness and death. In some ancient cultures, one out of every three babies died before the age of one. Sometimes diseases spread through ancient cities and killed large numbers of people. In A.D. 542, plague killed about half the population of Constantinople (modern-day Istanbul, Turkey). Ancient people saw death up close. Many people died at home. Their family members prepared their bodies for burial or cremation.

Although illness and death were familiar to them, ancient people were just as eager as modern people to live healthy lives. When people got sick or injured, they sought out someone to make them well. All ancient societies had healers or physicians. Some ancient societies even had hospitals and medical schools.

LEARNING FROM THE PAST

Archaeologists are scientists who study the remains of past cultures. To learn about ancient health and medicine, archaeologists must piece together many clues. Some clues come from ancient human bones. Archaeologists can study them to learn how tall ancient people were, whether they had bone disease, or even how old they were when they died.

Archaeologists also learn about ancient health and medicine by studying mummies. Mummies are dead bodies that have been preserved. The most famous mummies come from ancient Egypt. Scientists can examine the contents of a mummy's stomach to find out what food the person ate before he or she died. They can look in the mummy's intestines for germs that might have made the person sick. Scientists can also test a mummy's skin, hair, or teeth to learn whether the person suffered from a certain illness. In 2010 scientists tested tissue from the mummy of Tutankhamen, an ancient Egyptian king. The tests revealed that King Tut probably died from malaria, an insect-born disease.

▲ Archaeologists can learn a lot about ancient health and medicine by studying human remains. This archaeologist examines human bones from a catacomb, or underground cemetery, in Rome, Italy. People were buried there around A.D. 200 or 300.

In many cases, ancient people left clear clues about their health and medicine. Some ancient doctors wrote books about illness and medicine. Ancient paintings, drawings, and sculptures often show doctors or other healers at work. Archaeologists have found many ancient medical tools, such as surgeon's scalpels.

A LOT WITH A LITTLE

Ancient doctors did not have X-ray machines or microscopes. They did not have drugstores full of medicines. But they had just as much curiosity and creativity as modern doctors and scientists. With very few tools to help them, ancient healers accomplished great things.

More than ten thousand years ago, ancient healers made medicines from the bark, flowers, stems, leaves, and roots of plants. Doctors in ancient Peru and Bolivia performed brain surgery eight thousand years ago. Ancient Indian doctors performed plastic surgery more than two thousand years ago. Doctors in ancient Rome performed eye surgery. They removed cataracts, or cloudy lenses inside patients' eyes.

Ancient healers and doctors made many contributions to medical technology. This book tells the story of these contributions. Read on if you love surprises and the adventure of discovery. But beware! You'll also encounter a lot of blood and guts.

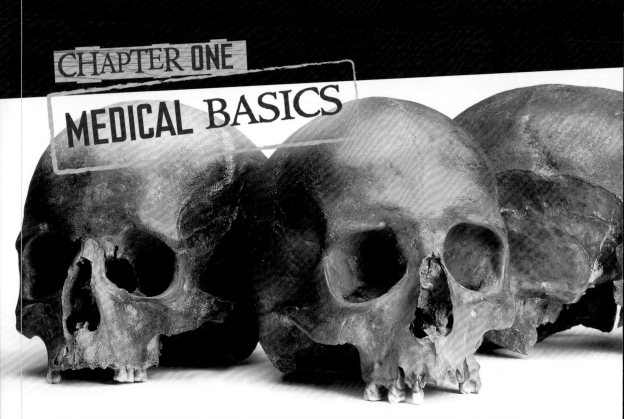

CHAPTER ONE

MEDICAL BASICS

▲ These ancient skulls come from what is now London, England. They date from the era of Roman rule there, from the 50s B.C. to the A.D. 400s. The skulls show that when these people were alive, they had diseased teeth.

The first humans on Earth lived about 2.5 million years ago. They were hunters and gatherers. They lived in small groups. They got their food by hunting game, fishing, and gathering wild plants. When the food in one area was all used up, the group moved to a new place. Hunter–gatherers made tools from stone, wood, animal bones, plant fibers, and clay.

FIRST AID

Like all people, early hunter–gatherers got into accidents and got sick. When studying ancient human skeletons, archaeologists often see signs of broken bones, tooth decay, gum disease, and arthritis. Some of these conditions were certainly very painful. How did early humans treat their ailments?

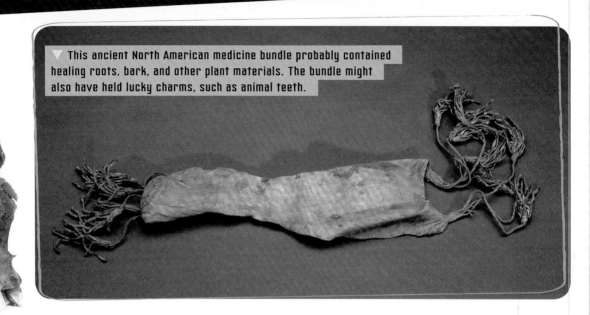

This ancient North American medicine bundle probably contained healing roots, bark, and other plant materials. The bundle might also have held lucky charms, such as animal teeth.

Some treatments probably came to ancient people naturally. When you feel pain, instinct tells you to rub the spot that hurts. When you cut your finger, your first reaction might be to grab the finger and squeeze it. The pressure tightens blood vessels in the finger and helps stop the bleeding. Early humans almost certainly used these kinds of simple treatments. They probably used hot stones to soothe their aches and pains.

Archaeologists have found ancient human bones that were fractured, or broken, but then healed. This evidence shows that ancient hunter–gatherers knew how to treat bone fractures. Ancient healers used splints, or supports, made of wood, bark, or other stiff material. The splints kept broken bones straight. They keep the bones from moving as they healed. They ensured that broken bones healed properly.

Early peoples probably discovered many remedies by accident. People ate figs because they were sweet. But people also noticed that figs are powerful laxatives, drugs that loosen the bowels. Early peoples saw the medical effects of plants such as figs. They passed on their knowledge from generation to generation.

This illustration shows an Algonquian shaman, or medicine man. Algonquian-speaking peoples once lived throughout the eastern woodlands of North America. The shaman used medicinal plants as well as magic to cure sick people.

MAGIC CURES

Many ancient cultures believed in gods and spirits. They thought that supernatural beings caused thunder, lightning, wind, rain, and other natural events. Ancient peoples also thought that supernatural beings could cause sickness. If someone became ill, people often blamed evil spirits.

"That mighty . . . healer, Dianket;
Or Midac, who excelled his sire [father] in skill;
The maiden-leech [physician], Armedda, mightier yet.
Who knew the herbs to cure, the herbs to kill."

—ancient Celtic verse about Dianket, a medicine god, and his physician children Midac and Armedda

To fight evil spirits, ancient people often turned to shamans, also called witch doctors or sorcerers. Such people were thought to have supernatural powers. Shamans treated illness with magic and good luck charms. But they also used effective medicines made from roots, bark, and other parts of plants.

ANCIENT DRUG USE

In modern times, some people use illegal drugs such as marijuana and heroin. Marijuana comes from the leaves and stems of the cannabis plant. Heroin comes from opium poppies.

These drugs weren't always illegal. In ancient times, people in many cultures smoked opium to relieve pain, treat illnesses, and bring on sleep. Farmers in southwestern Europe grew opium poppies as early as 6000 B.C. Archaeologists have found ancient opium pipes. They have also found ancient statues, jewelry, and other objects depicting opium poppies. Ancient people used cannabis fibers to make rope and textiles. But they also smoked marijuana and drank marijuana tea to treat aching joints, anxiety, and other ailments. The world's oldest marijuana pipes date to about 3000 B.C. They come from the ancient Kurgan culture of southeastern Europe.

Writers in ancient Greece, ancient China, and elsewhere wrote about opium and marijuana use. The writers noted that these drugs not only relieved certain ailments but also altered the mind. In modern times, fifteen U.S. states allow people to use marijuana for medical purposes. And many modern painkilling drugs are opiates (based on opium).

DYING YOUNG

Ancient healers were skilled at treating simple injuries and illnesses. But they were unable to treat most complicated health problems. Early humans regularly died from infections, wounds, and diseases. Many women died during childbirth.

In the modern United States, with the help of good food and modern medicine, men can expect to live to about the age of seventy-six. Women can expect to live to the age of eighty-one. Ancient hunter-gatherers had a

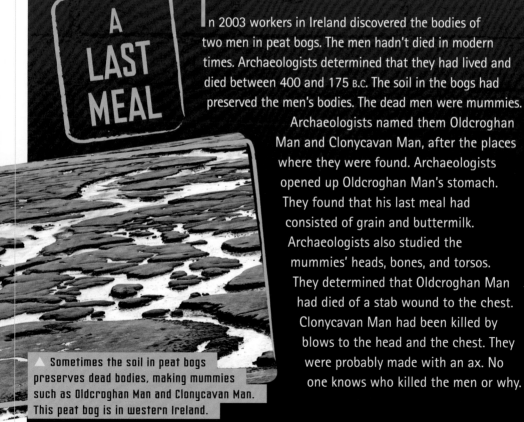

A LAST MEAL

In 2003 workers in Ireland discovered the bodies of two men in peat bogs. The men hadn't died in modern times. Archaeologists determined that they had lived and died between 400 and 175 B.C. The soil in the bogs had preserved the men's bodies. The dead men were mummies. Archaeologists named them Oldcroghan Man and Clonycavan Man, after the places where they were found. Archaeologists opened up Oldcroghan Man's stomach. They found that his last meal had consisted of grain and buttermilk. Archaeologists also studied the mummies' heads, bones, and torsos. They determined that Oldcroghan Man had died of a stab wound to the chest. Clonycavan Man had been killed by blows to the head and the chest. They were probably made with an ax. No one knows who killed the men or why.

▲ Sometimes the soil in peat bogs preserves dead bodies, making mummies such as Oldcroghan Man and Clonycavan Man. This peat bog is in western Ireland.

much shorter life span. The average male hunter-gatherer lived to only the age of thirty-five. The average female lived to the age of thirty.

HUMANS SETTLE DOWN

About ten thousand years ago, some people in the Middle East abandoned the hunter-gatherer lifestyle. They settled down and became farmers. Small farming settlements grew into towns. Towns eventually became cities.

Historians think that early farmers and city dwellers weren't as healthy as peoples who hunted and gathered. In towns and cities, many people lived close together. More people meant more chances for germs to spread. In addition, farming peoples raised animals such as cows, pigs, goats, chickens, and sheep. Sometimes the animals spread diseases to humans.

In ancient towns, people often dumped human waste into rivers. Germs grew in the rivers. People who drank the dirty river water got sick. Sometimes ancient townspeople piled up food waste and other garbage in big trash heaps. The trash attracted flies and other insects. The insects carried disease. The situation was better in hunter-gatherer societies. Small groups of hunter-gatherers did not heavily pollute rivers or create big piles of garbage. Hunter-gatherers rarely stayed in one place for long. They were always on the move, looking for fresh sources of food and clean drinking water.

CHAPTER TWO

ANCIENT EGYPT

The first written accounts of ancient medical technology come from Egypt. The ancient Egyptians left detailed medical records. They were almost like modern medical textbooks. Scribes, or trained writers, wrote down the texts on long scrolls of papyrus. Papyrus is a kind of paper made from reeds. Some of the scrolls were more than 6 feet (1.8 meters) long. They had writing on both sides. Ancient Egyptian scribes used a type of picture–writing called hieroglyphics.

Archaeologists have found Egyptian medical papyruses in ancient tombs. The best known are the Kahun Papyrus, the Edwin Smith Papyrus, and the Ebers Papyrus. The Kahun Papyrus was written around 1900 B.C. It deals with

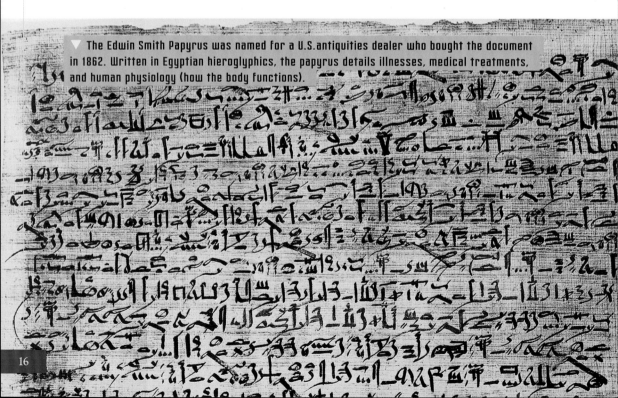

▼ The Edwin Smith Papyrus was named for a U.S. antiquities dealer who bought the document in 1862. Written in Egyptian hieroglyphics, the papyrus details illnesses, medical treatments, and human physiology (how the body functions).

childbirth and gynecology, the health care for women's reproductive systems. The Edwin Smith Papyrus, written about 1600 B.C., deals with surgery and the treatment of injuries. The Ebers Papyrus, written around 1500 B.C., is the most famous. It is an ancient medical encyclopedia. It told ancient Egyptian doctors how to diagnose, or recognize, certain illnesses. It told doctors how to treat the same illnesses. It told them how to prepare remedies. It also described how the heart and other human organs function.

THE FIRST KNOWN PHYSICIAN

Who was the world's first physician? It might have been an ancient Egyptian named Imhotep. Imhotep lived in the 2600s B.C. He was a man of many talents. He was chief assistant to the Egyptian pharaoh (king) Djoser.

Imhotep designed the first pyramid in Egypt, the Step Pyramid at Saqqara. In addition, Imhotep made medicines from plants. He used these remedies to treat people suffering from appendicitis, arthritis, and other ailments. The Egyptians later worshipped Imhotep as a god.

▶ This anicent Egyptian limestone statue shows Imhotep, one of the first physicians known by name. Imhotep also worked as an architect and as assistant to an Egyptian king in the 2600s B.C.

Hesy-re is another candidate for world's first physician. He lived in Egypt around 2600 B.C. He worked as "Chief of Physicians and Dentists to the pyramid builders." Egyptian writings say that Hesy-re operated on infected teeth and gums. He drilled holes into patients' gums. This procedure allowed pus to drain from the infection.

AHEAD OF THE REST

People in other ancient cultures thought that Egypt had the best medical care. Foreign rulers wrote to Egyptian pharaohs. The rulers asked for Egyptian doctors to visit them. The ancient Greek poet Homer wrote *The Odyssey* in the 700s B.C. In this epic, or long poem, Homer talked about Egyptian medical care. He described powerful drugs that an Egyptian doctor gave to a Greek queen. Homer noted that "in medical knowledge the Egyptian leaves the rest of the world behind."

Ancient Egypt had the first medical specialists. Specialists are doctors who treat specific illnesses or certain parts of the body. The Greek historian Herodotus wrote that "the practice of medicine they [the Egyptians] split into separate parts, each doctor being responsible for the treatment of only one disease."

▲ Originally painted in a tomb, this picture shows an ancient Egyptian doctor treating a patient. The original picture dates from 1292 to 1190 B.C. Later, an artist copied the scene on papyrus *(above)*.

READY FOR THE AFTERLIFE

▲ This Egyptian mummy and coffin come from the 1000s or 900s B.C. The mummy is now at the British Museum in London, England.

The ancient Egyptians believed in an afterlife—or life after death. They wanted to enter the afterlife with their bodies intact. To keep dead bodies from decaying, the ancient Egyptians turned them into mummies. In the process of mummifying bodies, mummy makers learned a lot about human anatomy.

By about 1500 B.C., the ancient Egyptians had perfected the mummy-making process. The steps were as follows:

• Remove the dead person's stomach, liver, lungs, intestines, and brain (but leave the heart in place).
• Cover the body with natron (a kind of salt) to dry it out.
• Treat the dried body with resins, oil, and wax to seal it against moisture.
• Stuff the body with straw or another substance to make it look more lifelike.
• Apply perfumes to the body.
• Wrap the body in linen bandages.
• Place the body in a coffin or a series of coffins (sometimes shaped and decorated to look like the person in life).
• Place the coffin in a tomb.

Mummy makers also preserved the dead person's organs and placed them in storage jars. The jars went into people's tombs alongside their coffins. The ancient Egyptians also mummified certain animals associated with their gods. These animals included baboons, jackals (a kind of dog), and rams. Sometimes the Egyptians turned pet cats and dogs into mummies and buried them with their owners.

"If thou examinest a man having a split in his cheek, shouldst thou find that there is a swelling, protruding and red, on the outside of that split . . . thou shouldst bind it with fresh meat the first day. His treatment is sitting until its swelling is reduced. Thou shalt treat it afterward [with] grease, honey, [and] lint every day until he recovers."

—Edwin Smith Papyrus, circa 1600 B.C.

Female doctors may have been common in ancient Egypt. A female doctor named Peseshet lived in Egypt around 2500 B.C. She is the first female physician known by name. Peseshet's title, "Lady Overseer of Lady Physicians," tells us that she was one of many female doctors.

MRHT, BYT, AND FTT

Mrht, *byt*, and *ftt* are the ancient Egyptian words for "grease," "honey," and "lint." Those were the ingredients of a popular Egyptian salve, or ointment. Doctors used the salve to treat cuts, scrapes, and other wounds. This ancient ointment really worked.

The grease might have been fat from an ox or another animal. It would have helped keep bandages from sticking to wounds. Honey was an ingredient in more Egyptian medicines than any other substance. As modern scientists know, honey can destroy bacteria, tiny organisms that can cause disease. Lint is fiber from cotton or another plant. The lint in Egyptian salve drew pus and other fluids out of wounds. It also helped bind together the other ingredients in the salve. The Egyptians often applied lint on its own to cuts to stop the bleeding.

EGYPTIAN SURGERY

Egyptian doctors did little or no major surgery. But they did perform minor surgery. They lanced, or pierced, boils (inflammations on the skin). They stitched up battle wounds. Another common procedure was circumcision. This is removal of the flap of skin at the end of a man's or boy's penis. The world's first known picture of surgery was carved on the wall of an Egyptian tomb around 2250 B.C. The picture shows doctors performing a circumcision.

The first Egyptian surgeons used knives made from flint, a type of stone, or obsidian, a kind of glass. These tools were razor sharp. Surgeons also used sharp "disposable" blades made from the stems of dried reeds. By 1500 B.C., Egyptian surgeons were using metal knives and other surgical tools.

A picture from an Egyptian temple shows about forty Egyptian medical instruments. The picture shows scales for weighing medicines and containers for holding solid and liquid medicines. It shows forceps, tweezerlike tools used for grasping body parts and foreign objects such as splinters. It shows hooks for spreading open incisions and wounds. It shows looped instruments for scraping away infected tissue.

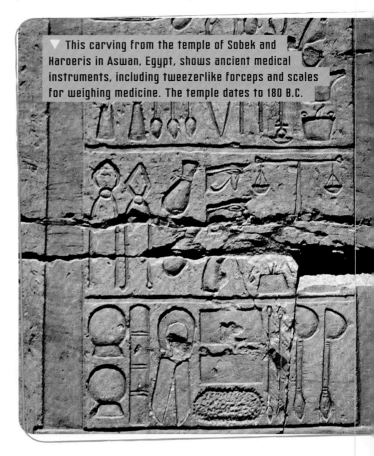

▼ This carving from the temple of Sobek and Haroeris in Aswan, Egypt, shows ancient medical instruments, including tweezerlike forceps and scales for weighing medicine. The temple dates to 180 B.C.

TOOTHISTS

Egypt is a dry, sandy place. In ancient Egypt, sand blew into people's homes. It blew into food and often got into people's mouths. The sand acted like sandpaper. It quickly wore away the hard coating of enamel on people's teeth. It exposed the teeth's inner nerves and blood vessels. People probably got horrible toothaches in ancient Egypt.

Studies of mummies show that tooth decay became a bigger and bigger problem as Egyptian society grew larger. As farming and trade increased in ancient Egypt, people ate a greater variety of foods. These foods included more sweets, which led to more tooth decay.

Dentists, called toothists or toothworkers, were important in ancient Egypt. Egyptian dentists did not treat toothaches in the easiest way, by pulling unhealthy teeth. Instead, they applied medicines to the teeth. They sometimes used magic spells to cure toothaches. Egyptian dentists also tried to keep loose adult teeth from falling out. They wrapped pieces of fine gold wire around loose teeth. They fastened the wire to other teeth to hold it in place.

▼ This wooden panel is from the tomb of Hesy-re, known as "Chief of Physicians and Dentists to the pyramid builders." He is shown next to dental and medical tools. The tomb dates to 2700–2600 B.C.

FRESH BREATH, EGYPTIAN STYLE

In modern times, many toothpastes contain baking soda. This substance helps clean the teeth and freshen the breath. The ancient Egyptians used baking soda more than four thousand years ago. To sweeten their breath, they chewed lumps of natron. This natural salt contains baking soda. It is found in deposits throughout Egypt.

The Egyptians also used elaborate mouth rinses, much like modern mouthwashes. One popular rinse was made of frankincense, goose fat, cumin (a spice), honey, and water. Instead of toothbrushes, ancient Egyptians might have cleaned their teeth with the frayed ends of twigs.

TREATMENTS THAT WORKED AND TREATMENTS THAT DIDN'T

The ancient Egyptians used drugs made from plants and animals. They used castor oil, which comes from castor beans, as a laxative. They used gel from the leaves of aloe plants to treat skin conditions. They drank a tea made from pomegranate bark to kill worms in the intestines. These remedies were all effective. Modern people still use them.

Many medicines and treatments from ancient Egypt did not work, however. For instance, the Egyptians used dead mice in medicines for toothaches, earaches, and other conditions. Sometimes doctors mashed the mouse into a paste and mixed it with other ingredients. Sometimes they simply put a dead mouse right onto an

Castor oil comes from castor beans (below). People in ancient Egypt used castor oil as a laxative, just as modern people do.

aching tooth or swollen gum. Did the dead mouse treatments work? Probably not. They might have even made the patient sicker.

Ancient Egyptian physicians developed the first known treatment for baldness. The Ebers Papyrus directed mixing together the fat of a lion, a hippopotamus, a crocodile, a cat, a snake, and an ibex (a wild goat) and applying the mixture to a bald person's head. Chances are, this treatment didn't work either.

MEDICINE IN MESOPOTAMIA

East of Egypt, a number of ancient cultures flourished between the Tigris and Euphrates rivers. This region is called Mesopotamia, which means "between rivers" in ancient Greek. It covers parts of present-day Iraq, Syria, and Turkey.

The ancient peoples of Mesopotamia wrote a lot about religion, law, and business. They wrote much less about medicine. The scant writings reveal that medicine in ancient Mesopotamia was partly based on sorcery. People believed that angry gods and spirits caused sickness. When people got sick, they often sought out an *ashipu*, or a sorcerer. Sorcerers used charms and magic spells to make people well.

Sometimes sick people in ancient Mesopotamia visited an *asu*, or a physician. Asus performed minor surgery, such as cutting into wounds to drain pus. They also prescribed remedies made from plants.

One common treatment for injury in ancient Mesopotamia was a plaster, or a poultice. To make a plaster, the asu combined healing ingredients such as plant remedies, spices, honey, and animal fat. The asu then applied the mixture to a cloth. He wrapped it around the patient's injured limb or wound. Modern studies show that some ancient Mesopotamian plasters might have been effective. They might have kept germs from growing in wounds.

FROM BALSAM TO BALM

In modern times, we use spices to liven up our food. We burn incense to make our homes smell good or to mask bad smells. We wear perfume to make our bodies smell good. People in ancient Egypt used spices, incense, and perfumes for these same purposes. But they also used them as medicine.

The Bible talks about the "balm of Gilead." This balm was actually balsam from balsam trees, much like this one in modern-day Jordan. Ancient people used balsam to treat colds and coughs.

Ancient peoples figured that if something smelled good, it was probably good for you. They were often right. Balsam is a fragrant, oily substance that flows from Balsam fir trees and other kinds of trees and plants. People in Egypt used balsam to treat colds and coughs. The modern word *balm*, which refers to a healing ointment, comes from the Latin word for "balsam." A place called Gilead, in modern-day Jordan, was famous in ancient times for its balsam fir trees and its healing balms.

The ancient Egyptians imported vast quantities of myrrh from the Arabian Peninsula. Myrrh comes from the resin of myrrh trees. (Resin is a sticky substance found in plants.) The ancient Egyptians used this pleasant-smelling substance as a perfume and as incense. They also used myrrh in wound salves. Modern doctors have found that myrrh is a mild antiseptic—a substance that inhibits the growth of germs.

CHAPTER THREE

ANCIENT INDIA

People in India first established cities in about 2500 B.C. They settled in the valley along the Indus River, in modern-day Pakistan and western India. The valley was home to cities such as Mohenjo-Daro and Harappa. Around 1500 B.C., people from central Asia moved south into India. They developed the Hindu religion and a language called Sanskrit. People in ancient India also developed advanced medical technology.

KNOWLEDGE OF LIFE

Ancient Indian medicine was called ayurveda. This term means "science of life" or "knowledge of life." The Sanskrit word for physician was *vaidya*, or "one who has wisdom."

Much of our knowledge about ancient Indian medicine comes from two books: the *Charaka Samhita* and the *Sushruta Samhita*. (*Samhita* means "collection" in Sanskrit.) One book was written by a doctor named Charaka. The other was written by a surgeon named Sushruta. Nobody knows exactly when these men lived and when their books were written. The *Charaka Samhita* might date to around 300 B.C. Sushruta's book dates to around A.D. 100.

Both books provide extensive information on diseases, remedies, childbirth, and other medical

issues. They also offer advice on healthy living. The books explain the benefits of a good diet, lots of sleep, cleanliness, and exercise. Sushruta's book gives detailed information on surgical treatments. For insomniacs, or people who couldn't get a good night's sleep, Sushruta gave this guidance:

The following measures are useful in cases of sleeplessness— such as anointing the body, rubbing of oil on the head, soft massages of the body (with cleansing paste) and shampooing; a diet consisting of cakes and pastry made up of . . . rice and wheat

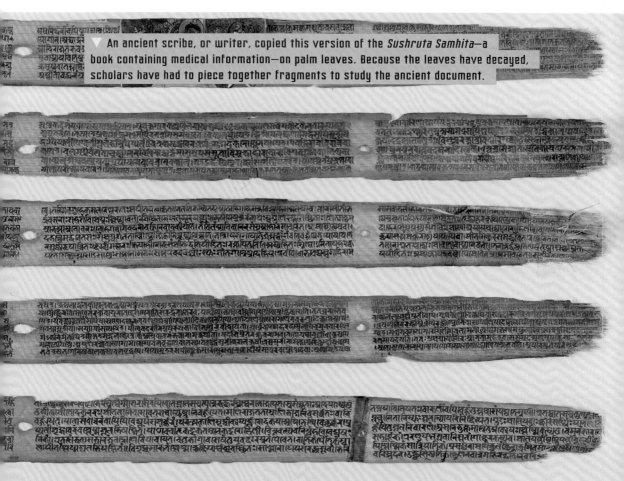

An ancient scribe, or writer, copied this version of the *Sushruta Samhita*—a book containing medical information—on palm leaves. Because the leaves have decayed, scholars have had to piece together fragments to study the ancient document.

prepared with sugar or other derivatives of sugar–cane, sweet or soothing articles with milk or meat juice . . . and eating of grapes, sugar and sugar–cane at night, are beneficial (in such cases); so also a soft and pleasant bed, and easy and convenient seats and means of [travel].

"A bite by a scorpion of this species is accompanied by pain [in the seat of the bite], shivering, numbness of the limbs and a flow of blackish blood [from the punctures of the bite]. In the case of a bite at any of the extremities, the pain courses upward, accompanied by a burning sensation, perspiration, swelling of the bitten part and fever."

—*Sushruta Samhita*, ca. A.D. 100

PLASTIC SURGERY

Plastic surgery might seem like modern technology. But Indian doctors performed plastic surgery several thousand years ago. They sometimes treated people whose faces had been disfigured in accidents or warfare.

Perhaps a soldier had lost a nose in battle. To create a new nose, the surgeon cut a triangular flap of skin and tissue from the patient's forehead. The surgeon lifted the wide end of the flap free from the forehead. He left the narrow portion of the flap attached to the bridge of the patient's nose. The surgeon then twisted the flap skin side up. He folded it down over the nose opening and stitched it in place. The surgeon made new nostrils by wrapping the corners of the flap around two hollow tubes. Eventually, the skin of the new nose fused with the surrounding skin on the patient's face. In addition, new skin eventually grew over the patient's forehead where the flap had been cut.

EARLOBE REPAIR

People in ancient India pierced their ears. Not only that, they stretched their earlobes into long loops. Then they hung heavy ornaments from the openings. The practice was thought to protect against "the evil influences of . . . stars and spirits." Ear piercing and stretching took place in childhood. A doctor pierced a child's earlobes with a sharp needle or another pointed tool. The doctor plugged the piercings with wads of cotton to enlarge them. Over the next few days, he inserted wooden plugs to make the holes even bigger. After the openings healed, people strung large, heavy earrings from the piercings.

▲ The ancient Indian practice of plugging and stretching the earlobes continues into modern times. The practice is thought to ward off evil spirits. This man from modern India displays stretched earlobes and a traditional headdress.

Sometimes the heavy earrings tore people's earlobes into two long strands. Ancient Indian surgeons learned to repair the damage. The process was similar to the nose operation. It involved using a flap of skin from below the ear to create a new earlobe. Here is how Sushruta described the technology:

> A surgeon well-versed in the knowledge of surgery should slice off a patch of living flesh from the cheek [below the ear] of a person devoid of [without] ear-lobes in a manner so as to have one of its ends attached to the [face]. Then the part, where the artificial ear-lobe is to be made, should be slightly scarified [scratched with a knife] and the living flesh, full of blood and sliced off as previously described, should be [attached] to it.

ANT SUTURES

Indian surgeons sometimes encountered badly wounded patients, such as soldiers wounded in battle. Sometimes patients arrived with their intestines spilling out of a bloody stomach wound. If the intestines themselves were cut open, the surgeon had to repair them. The normal procedure was to suture (stitch up) the intestines using cotton, linen, silk, or another kind of thread.

But the operation was dangerous. The cloth stitches acted like wicks. They drew fluids out of the intestines. A tiny amount of such fluid, smaller than the period at the end of this sentence, contains millions of bacteria. Such bacteria can cause life-threatening infections.

To protect against infection, ancient Indian surgeons developed a clever solution. Before starting intestinal surgery, they collected giant black ants. Some were almost 1 inch (2.5 centimeters) long. These insects will clamp their powerful jaws around food, their animal enemies, or almost any other object they touch.

After operating on someone's intestines, a surgeon carefully held an ant at the edge of the incision and let it clamp down. The ant's jaws drew the cut edges of the intestines together. The surgeon placed another ant alongside the first. And another and another—until ant jaws sealed the entire incision. Even after the surgeon cut away the ants' bodies, the jaws stayed firmly clamped in place. Sushruta advised surgeons how to proceed next. He wrote: "After that the intestines with the heads of the ants attached to them should be gently pushed back into the [abdominal] cavity and reinstated in their original situation therein."

After that step, surgeons sewed up the patient's muscles and skin with a needle and ordinary cloth stitches. Within a few weeks, the patient's body would break down the ant jaws. The jaws turned into a harmless liquid. By that time, the intestines were safely healed.

TEACHING AIDS

Modern doctors spend a great deal of time practicing surgery. They must learn how hard to press down on scalpels and how tightly to pull on stitches. They practice on cadavers (dead human bodies) or animals rather than on

A GOOD GRASP

Ancient Indian surgeons used a wide assortment of instruments. The *Sushruta Samhita* lists more than 120 surgical instruments. These include scalpels, forceps, probes, saws, and needles. Indian toolmakers crafted forceps to look like the jaws of certain animals. The lion forceps had huge jaws. It was good for grasping big structures such as bones. The heron mouth forceps had long, narrow, sharply pointed jaws. Doctors used it to remove splinters and other objects from deep within wounds. Other ancient Indian forceps looked like the jaws of jackals, cats, blue jays, hawks, and crocodiles.

living people. Plastic models also help modern surgeons prepare for treating real patients.

Ancient Indian physicians also practiced on models. Student surgeons practiced making incisions on watermelons and cucumbers. They stitched up pieces of animal hide to practice suturing human tissue. Surgeons practiced amputating human limbs by cutting the limbs off dead animals. They practiced cautery, or burning wounds to prevent bleeding or infection, on pieces of fresh meat. Surgeons practiced the proper use of forceps by picking seeds out of different kinds of fruit.

SNAKEBITE

India is home to many poisonous snakes, including the deadly hooded cobra. In ancient India, vaidyas were skilled in treating bites of poisonous snakes. But they had to act quickly.

The bite of the hooded cobra is often deadly. But if an ancient vaidya acted quickly, he could save a snakebite victim.

Ancient Indian doctors used tongue scrapers *(above)* to remove disease-causing bacteria, fungi, and dead cells from patients' tongues. A finger knife *(right)* fit on a surgeon's index finger. He simply slid his finger across a patient's skin or tissue to cut it.

If the victim had been bitten on the leg, which was the most common spot, the vaidya tied a strip of cloth tightly around the leg, about 2 inches (5 cm) above the wound. This procedure squeezed the victim's veins. It helped keep the snake venom (poison) from spreading up the leg and into the rest of the body. Then, with a piece of linen cloth in his mouth, the vaidya sucked on the bite. He drew poison from the wound into the cloth. Next, he cut into the wound with a small knife. Then he cauterized the wound by pressing on it with a hot coal. Finally, he applied a healing plaster to the wound. If the vaidya didn't get to the victim quickly enough, however, the snake venom would kill the victim.

FIGHTING SMALLPOX

Many times in history, smallpox has swept through large regions. This disease, caused by a virus, has killed hundreds of millions of people. It has scarred or blinded many others.

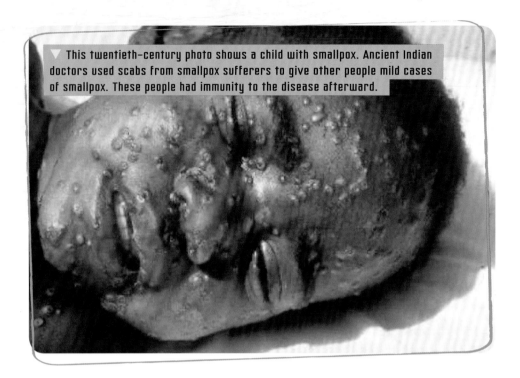
This twentieth-century photo shows a child with smallpox. Ancient Indian doctors used scabs from smallpox sufferers to give other people mild cases of smallpox. These people had immunity to the disease afterward.

Smallpox victims get a rash on the face and other parts of the body. At first the rash looks like thousands of small pimples. Then the pimples become larger and fill with pus. They break open and form crusty scabs. The scabs fall off. The patient is left with pitted scars called pocks. Smallpox was so common in some ancient societies that people stood out if their faces were *not* disfigured by pocks. After getting smallpox once, people develop lifelong immunity, or resistance, to the disease.

The ancient Indians found a way to protect people from smallpox. They used a technique called variolation. A doctor took dried scabs from patients with mild cases of smallpox. The doctor placed the scabs on the skin or inside the noses of healthy people. Sometimes, healthy people ate the scabs. The procedure exposed healthy people to a mild form of the smallpox virus. The virus made the people sick but usually did not kill them. After that, these people had lifelong immunity to smallpox. In some cases, however, people did get severe cases of smallpox after variolation. Some of these people died.

THE FIRST HOSPITALS

In many ancient societies, sick people remained at home. Sometimes healers or doctors visited them. Sometimes family members gave them treatments. But people in ancient India were the first ones to set up hospitals to care for sick people. An inscription carved into a slab of rock around 226 B.C. honored an Indian ruler named Ashoka. It praised him for building hospitals. Other records indicate that hospitals operated in modern–day Sri Lanka around 437 B.C. Sri Lanka is an island south of India in the Indian Ocean.

▼ When ancient people got sick, they usually stayed home. But the Indian ruler Ashoka had some hospitals built during his reign in the 200s B.C.

CHAPTER FOUR

ANCIENT CHINA

People in ancient China began farming between 5000 and 3000 B.C. The first farming villages were in the Yellow River valley in northern China. Gradually, the villages grew into big cities. The Yellow River provided water for drinking, irrigation (watering crops), and transportation. People also caught fish in the river. When the river flooded the land, it left behind layers of rich yellow soil. The soil was perfect for growing crops.

MAGICIANS AND PHYSICIANS

Early medicine in ancient China involved much magic and superstition. People believed that evil spirits caused sickness. People often consulted the spirits of their dead ancestors to seek out a cause of or a treatment for an illness.

But gradually, medical knowledge grew. As early as 2000 B.C., physicians were practicing their trade in China. They learned to diagnose disease by taking a patient's pulse, observing his or her skin color, and smelling his or her breath. They treated illness with herbal remedies, special diets, and massage. They also still employed magic spells and charms. Around 500 B.C., the Chinese philosopher Confucius wrote, "A man without persistence will never make a good magician or a good physician."

THE YELLOW EMPEROR'S CLASSIC

Much of our knowledge about ancient Chinese medicine comes from a book called the *Nei Ching*. In this book, a character called the Yellow

Emperor holds discussions with his prime minister, Ch'i Po. They discuss many aspects of human health and healing. They discuss human anatomy, disease, and physiology, or how the body functions.

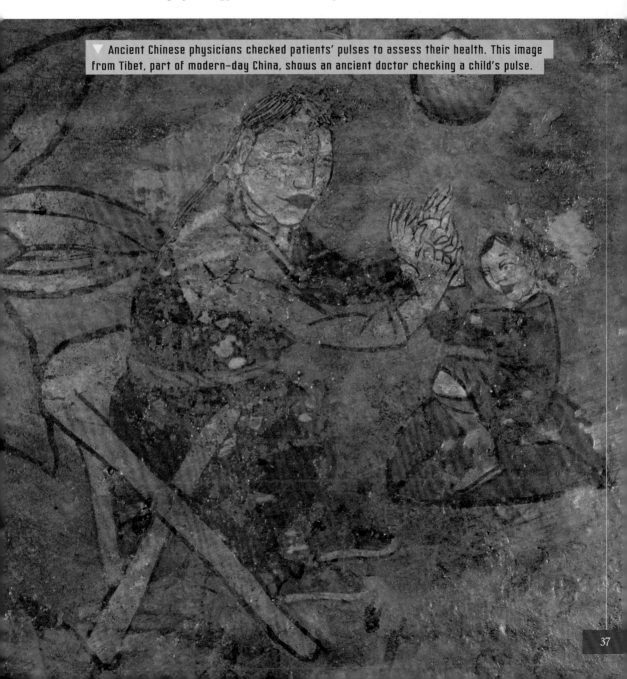

▼ Ancient Chinese physicians checked patients' pulses to assess their health. This image from Tibet, part of modern-day China, shows an ancient doctor checking a child's pulse.

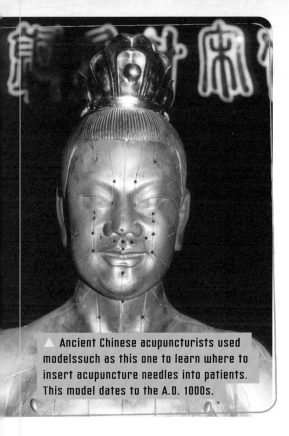

▲ Ancient Chinese acupuncturists used models such as this one to learn where to insert acupuncture needles into patients. This model dates to the A.D. 1000s.

The *Nei Ching* explains that good health is based on a balance of two life forces, yin and yang. Yin is a dark, moist, feminine force. Yang is a bright, dry, masculine force. These forces flow through the body along fourteen meridians, or channels. Sickness and pain result when yin and yang are out of balance. The *Nei Ching* tells how to restore this balance using a process called acupuncture. An acupuncturist inserts needles at various points along the body's meridians. The treatments balance out yin and yang.

The *Nei Ching* also describes a technique called moxibustion. This treatment involves burning small piles of moxa, an herb, on a patient's skin. The process increases the flow of warmth, blood, and energy inside the body. It too alleviates certain illnesses.

"When the pulse has a red appearance and there is [a stubborn] cough, the examiner says that there is amassed air within (the heart) and it is dangerous to eat at this particular time. This disease is known as 'numbness of the heart.' It is contracted through external evil influences, causing anxiety and emptying the heart while the evil influences follow into it."

—*Nei Ching*, ca. 479—300 B.C.

SOME HEALING PLANTS OF ANCIENT CHINA

Ancient Chinese doctors used hundreds of plants to make medicines. They usually boiled or soaked the plants in water to make tea. Some modern doctors still prescribe these remedies. You should not try them without consulting a doctor, however.

▼ Ginseng is used in modern times to treat medical ailments like high blood pressure. It can also be found in some energy drinks.

PLANT	PARTS USED TO MAKE MEDICINE	GOOD FOR TREATING
Astragalus	Roots	Allergies, digestive problems, skin disorders
Cinnamon	Twigs and bark	Poor blood circulation, allergies
Ginger	Rhizome (underground stem)	Digestive problems, nausea, coughs, colds
Ginseng	Roots	High blood pressure, fatigue
Licorice	Roots	Inflammation, digestive problems, hepatitis, sore throat
Peony	Roots	Poor blood circulation
Rhubarb	Roots	Constipation, poor appetite, pain
Salvia	Roots	Injuries, inflammation, infection, high blood pressure

The *Nei Ching* offers advice on diet. It says, "If too much salt is used for food, the pulse hardens." This is good advice. A "hardened" pulse means high blood pressure. Modern doctors know that eating a lot of salt can raise blood pressure. And high blood pressure increases a person's risk for heart attack and stroke.

The Yellow Emperor is a mysterious figure in Chinese history. Nobody knows exactly when he lived or whether he was real or legendary. Some historians think he lived around 2600 B.C. The *Nei Ching* probably was written down long after his death. Historians date the book to between 479 and 300 B.C.

MORE ABOUT ACUPUNCTURE

No one knows when acupuncture began in China. Archaeologists have found thin stone needles in ancient Chinese tombs. These might have been used to lance boils. But they might have been acupuncture needles.

By the time of the Yellow Emperor, acupuncture was a fully developed system of medicine in China. Instead of stone needles, Chinese acupuncturists used gold, silver, or bronze needles. In the following centuries, acupuncture became more and more systematic. Chinese doctors wrote many books on acupuncture, moxibustion, and the underlying philosophy of yin and yang.

▲ Ancient acupuncture needles look like ordinary straight pins like these old needles. In modern times, acupuncture is used around the world to treat pain and other conditions.

SPECIALISTS ABOUND

Like ancient Egypt, ancient China had medical specialists. A book called the *Chou Li* (Institutions of the Chou) describes the Chinese government during the Chou dynasty. This was a period of rule by the Chou family. The dynasty lasted from 1122 to 221 B.C.

The *Chou Li* lists the Chou emperor's staff. Staff members included a chief of physicians, food physicians (dietitians), physicians for simple diseases, ulcer physicians, and animal physicians (veterinarians). The book explains: "All the people belonging to the administration of the kingdom [the emperor's staff], who suffer from ordinary diseases, head diseases, or wounds, come to him [the chief of physicians]. Thereupon he orders the various physicians to share among them the treatment of these diseases." The physicians for simple diseases dealt with common ailments such as headaches, fevers, colds, and coughs. Physicians for ulcers handled more complicated matters such as wounds and internal bleeding.

CHAPTER FIVE

THE ANCIENT AMERICAS

▲ In North America, many groups carried on ancient medical traditions into modern times. For instance, Hupa people in California built this ancient-style sweathouse (sauna) in the early 1920s.

Ancient America was home to thousands of different cultures. People lived in the far north, near the North Pole, all the way down to the southernmost tip of South America. Some ancient Americans were hunter–gatherers. Others were farmers or city dwellers. In modern times, we sometimes use the term *Indian* to refer to all these people. But each group had its own name.

Like other ancient peoples, ancient Americans used some commonsense methods for maintaining good health. Many groups built saunas, or sweathouses. In these small huts, people built fires and heated rocks. They splashed water on the hot rocks to create steam. Sitting and sweating inside a sauna refreshed people both physically and mentally. Ancient Americans also used massage to treat aches and pains.

Alder trees such as this one gave ancient North Americans many different remedies. People used alder bark to treat stomach cramps, swelling, and skin problems. Alder berries treated fever and diarrhea.

THE AMERICAN MEDICINE CABINET

Each ancient American group used its own plant remedies. The ingredients depended on what grew in the region. Alder trees are common in North America. The Penobscot Indians, who lived in modern–day Maine, drank alder bark tea for stomach cramps. The Potawatomi Indians of the Great Lakes region rubbed alder bark juice on their skin to relieve itching. The nearby Menominee Indians used alder bark to reduce swelling. Other North American groups used alder berries to treat fever and diarrhea.

Sassafras trees, which grow in eastern North America, provided more medicines. Ancient North Americans used sassafras root to treat fevers, sassafras leaves for bruises, and sassafras berries for pain. Many American groups used balsam to treat colds, coughs, and asthma. Some groups used cedar bark for headaches and muscle aches. Slippery elm trees provided a remedy for digestive problems. Goldenseal root was good for sore eyes. Witch hazel trees offered remedies for bruises, sprains, and skin problems.

THE HEALER'S ART

Beside plant remedies, ancient American healers used a number of other treatments. Bloodletting, also called bleeding, was a common practice in the ancient Americas and elsewhere. Healers cut patients in an area of pain or illness and let some of their blood flow out. The point was to heal a patient by removing "bad blood."

Cautery was also widespread in the ancient world. Healers burned wounds to stop their bleeding. Some Indian groups used cautery to treat stomach pains. One British writer in North America observed:

> They [Indians in North Carolina] cure the Spleen . . . by burning with a Reed. They lay the Patient on his Back, so put a hollow Cane into the Fire, where they run the End thereof till it is very hot, and on Fire at the end. Then they lay a Piece of thin Leather on the Patient's Belly, between the pit of the stomach and the Navel, so press the hot Reed on the leader, which burns the Patient so that you may ever after see the Impression of the Reed where it was laid on. . . . This is used for the Belly-Ach sometimes.

Indian healers were skilled when it came to setting broken bones. They packed cloth or wet clay around a broken limb before applying a splint. This extra padding helped support the broken bone as it healed. The Ojibwa people of Minnesota and Wisconsin used cedar wood to make splints. The Pima Indians of modern-day Arizona made splints from the ribs of giant cactuses.

MAGIC AND MEDICINE

In many ancient American societies, disease and medicine were intertwined with the spirit world. People thought that witches, spirits, and ghosts could cause illness and other misfortunes. So ancient American healers had to be skilled in

ANCIENT BRAIN SURGERY

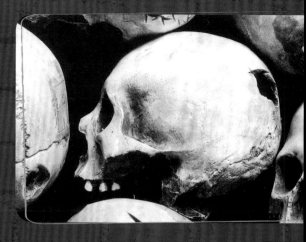

In 1867 a French brain surgeon, Paul Broca, ran his hands over a four-thousand-year-old skull. An archaeologist had found the skull in central France. It looked like someone had cut a big chunk of bone from the skull and polished the rim around the hole. Broca quickly realized that the rim had not been polished. The smooth edge actually was new bone tissue. As bone heals after an injury, fresh tissue grows in the cracks and pores. That growth results in a smooth, shiny appearance.

There could be no doubt. The hole had been made in the skull of a living person. The skull belonged to a patient who had undergone brain surgery thousands of years earlier. And the patient had lived long enough afterward for the bone to begin healing.

The French skull was not a unique example. Archaeologists began to find more ancient skulls with drilled holes. Examples came from all over the world, but most *(above)* came from ancient Peru. How and why had the ancient Peruvians performed brain surgery?

Cutting or drilling a hole in a skull is called trepanation. Ancient surgeons used the technique to relieve pressure on the brain after a head injury. They might have also used it to release "evil spirits" from the heads of mentally ill people. To make the holes, ancient surgeons used razor-sharp stone knives or drills. They probably gave patients a powerful drug, such as cocaine, to dull the pain of the operation.

Brain surgery is dangerous. Even in modern times, people can get infections after brain surgery and die. But the new bone growth on the ancient trepanned skulls shows that many patients survived surgery and lived long enough to heal. Some studies indicate that three out of four ancient trepanation patients survived. In some skulls, the healing is extensive. These patients must have lived for years after surgery.

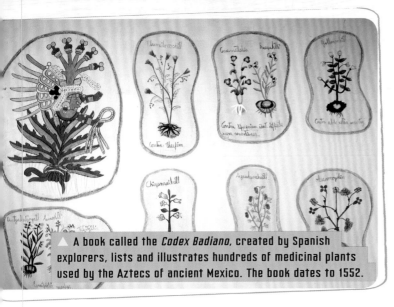

A book called the *Codex Badiano*, created by Spanish explorers, lists and illustrates hundreds of medicinal plants used by the Aztecs of ancient Mexico. The book dates to 1552.

several ways. They had to know how to use plant remedies and other medicines. But they also had to communicate with spirits to cure or prevent illness.

When someone got sick, ancient Americans often assumed that evil spirits were to blame. It was the job of the shaman to withdraw those spirits. Often shamans used magic spells to remove the spirits. But sometimes they sucked the spirits from the patient directly using a hollow animal bone, a stone, or a stick. At least, people *believed* the shaman was sucking out evil spirits. In reality, he or she sucked infected blood, snake venom, or pus from the patient's body. Sucking out the poison or infection often helped the sick person recover.

"As there are in this country many poysonous Herbs and Creatures, so the Indian People have excellent Skill in applying [effective] Antidotes [cures] to them; for Medicinal Herbs are here found in great Plenty, the Woods and Savannas [grasslands] being their [druggists'] Shops, from whence they fetch Herbs, Leaves, Barks of Trees, with which they make all their Medicines, and perform notable Cures."

— John Brickell, British physician in North Carolina, 1737

Ancient American healers used a number of tools in their work. They used smooth stones to grind up plants to make medicine. To inject medicine into patients, they used syringes. These tools were made from hollow bones and animal bladders. Some equipment had more to do with magic than hands–on medicine. American healers often played drums and rattles to communicate with the spirit world. They sometimes wore scary masks and costumes to frighten away evil spirits. Some ancient American healers carried a medicine bundle made of animal skins. The bundle held charms and magical objects, such as deer tails and snake bones.

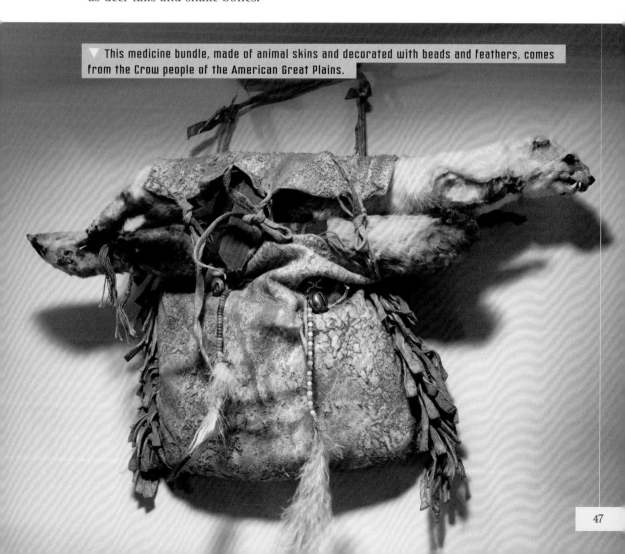

▼ This medicine bundle, made of animal skins and decorated with beads and feathers, comes from the Crow people of the American Great Plains.

NEWCOMERS FROM THE EAST

Cinchona trees grow on the eastern slopes of the Andes Mountains of South America. The bark of these trees contains a medicine called quinine. Ancient South Americans ground the bark into powder. They mixed it in hot water to make medicine. The medicine was effective in reducing fevers.

When Europeans came to South America in the 1500s, they brought diseases that people of the Americas had not been exposed to before. One of these diseases was malaria. Malaria makes people feverish and sickens them in a number of ways. The disease is often deadly. When

▲ Ancient peoples of the South American Andes used the bark of the *cinchona* tree to treat fevers. When Spanish explorers arrived in the Andes in the 1500s, they realized that *cinchona* bark was an effective treatment for malaria.

this new disease arrived in their area, ancient South Americans naturally turned to *cinchona* bark, which they knew to be effective in treating fevers. As it turned out, the quinine inside the bark was a powerful treatment for malaria. This discovery pleased the Europeans, who had no effective malaria drugs in their homelands. Europeans rushed to South America to collect *cinchona* bark and ship it back to Europe.

Malaria was not the only disease that Europeans brought to the Americas. European explorers, settlers, and soldiers also brought smallpox, measles, typhus, diphtheria, mumps, tuberculosis, and yellow fever. Because ancient Americans hadn't been exposed to these diseases, their bodies hadn't built up any immunity against them. Shamans found that their plant remedies and magic were powerless against these illnesses. Epidemics of smallpox and other diseases killed American Indians by the hundreds and sometimes by the thousands.

Europeans also went to war with many Indian peoples for control of land. The Europeans killed some Indians and enslaved others. But European diseases killed far more ancient Americans than warfare did. Some historians think that diseases from Europe wiped out about 90 percent of the ancient native American population.

CHAPTER SIX

ANCIENT GREECE

Ancient Greece was home to famous writers, philosophers, scientists, and artists. It was a center of learning in the ancient world. Not surprisingly, ancient Greece was also home to skilled doctors. Many modern medical traditions have their roots in ancient Greece.

THE GOD OF MEDICINE

As in many ancient societies, medicine and religion were intertwined in ancient Greece. People thought that gods could both cause and cure illness. The Greeks worshipped a god of healing named Asclepius. They prayed to him when they got sick or when epidemics of disease swept through Greek cities. According to Greek myth, Asclepius learned the art of healing from his father, the god Apollo. Asclepius's children included Hygeia, the goddess of health, cleanliness, and sanitation, and Panacea, the goddess of healing. Asclepius's symbol was a snake coiled around a staff.

The ancient Greeks built temples in honor of Asclepius. The temples were part health spa, part house of worship. Sick people went there to be cured and also to pray to Asclepius. Patients hoped that Asclepius would appear to them in a dream and administer a "dream drug" or "dream surgery." Priests at the temples also treated patients with special diets, massage, and plant medicines.

The health temples were usually built near mineral springs, where mineral-rich water flowed from underground. People believed that bathing in or drinking the waters would cure illness. The temple to Asclepius in Pergamum, in modern-day Turkey, had a mineral spring at its center. One Roman writer described the curative powers of the water there:

This marble carving from the fourth century B.C. shows Asclepius caring for a patient. Asclepius was the Greek god of healing. Sick people hoped he would heal them through their dreams.

This [spring] was discovered by and belongs to the great miracle–worker [Asclepius], he who does everything for the healthy [well–being] of humankind and for many it [the water] takes the place of drugs. For many who have bathed in it recovered their eyesight, while many by drinking were cured of chest ailments and regained vital breathing. For in some cases it cured their feet, while for others it cured some other part of the body.

If the waters at Pergamum sound too good to be true, they probably were. No doubt, soaking in the mineral waters relieved people's aches and pains. But stories of miracle cures were most likely exaggerated.

THE FATHER OF MEDICINE

Hippocrates was the most famous physician of ancient times. As a physician and a professor of medicine in ancient Greece, he took a scientific approach to treating patients. He taught medical students to carefully observe each patient's symptoms and to select an appropriate treatment. His contributions to medicine later earned him the label the Father of Medicine.

Hippocrates was born around 460 B.C. on the Greek island of Cos. The

WHAT KIND OF PLAGUE?

The Great Plague of Athens struck Greece between 430 and 425 B.C. The plague killed up to three hundred thousand people in Athens and other parts of Greece. This was about 25 percent of the Greek population. In his book *The History of the Peloponnesian War*, the Greek historian Thucydides described the plague. He said that victims suddenly got high fevers and sore throats. Blisters broke out on their skin. They vomited, had diarrhea, and suffered from intense thirst. "The bodies of dying men lay one upon the other," Thucydides wrote, "and half-dead creatures reeled about the streets and gathered round all the fountains in their longing for water." Some victims developed hiccups that would not stop. At the same time, the epidemic struck other parts of the ancient world, including the city of Rome.

The plague is caused by the bacterium *Yersinia pestis*. This was the disease that struck the people of Constantinople in A.D. 542. But the Great Plague of Athens was not necessarily caused by *Yersinia pestis*. Ancient writers often used the term *plague* to describe any widespread epidemic. The epidemic in Athens might have been an actual plague, or it might have been another disease. Medical historians have long debated which disease it was.

island already had a temple to honor Asclepius. Hippocrates established a medical school as part of the temple complex.

To learn about medicine in Hippocrates' time, modern scholars look to a series of about seventy medical essays. No one knows who wrote the essays. Hippocrates or other doctors at Cos might have written some of them. These essays tell us a lot about medicine in ancient Greece. Because they are associated with Hippocrates, modern physicians call the writings the Hippocratic Collection.

In 1996 researchers in California came up with a theory. They argued that the Great Plague of Athens was an epidemic of Ebola virus. Ebola caused alarm in 1995 when it killed 242 people in the nation in Africa currently called the Democratic Republic of Congo. The researchers said that Ebola symptoms and the plague symptoms reported by Thucydides were very similar. Thucydides said that victims could not stop hiccupping. Ebola also causes severe hiccupping in many of its victims. In addition, African green monkeys transmit the Ebola virus to humans. Not far from modern Athens, archaeologists have found ancient wall paintings showing African green monkeys. Greek traders must have brought the monkeys back with them after voyages to Africa. Perhaps the monkey brought Ebola to Athens.

Not all scientists agreed with the Ebola theory. They noted that Thucydides' medical descriptions were imprecise and couldn't be counted on as solid evidence. They noted other flaws in the Ebola theory.

The search for the cause of the outbreak continued. In 2006 Greek researchers studied human remains from an ancient burial pit in Athens. The remains dated to the years of the Great Plague. The researchers analyzed the teeth of some of the skeletons. They found evidence that typhoid fever had killed the plague victims.

But some scientists found problems with this theory too. The puzzle of the Great Plague of Athens remains a topic of debate among both scientists and historians.

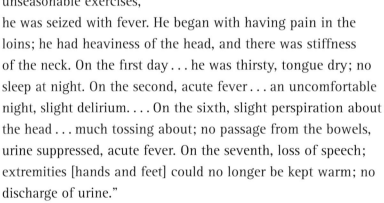

Of all Hippocrates' contributions to medicine, the use of case histories might be the most important. Hippocrates kept a case history on each patient. He described the patient's symptoms, his own diagnosis, the treatment he prescribed, and the outcome of the treatment. One case history began:

Silenus lived on the Broad–way. . . . From fatigue, drinking, and unseasonable exercises, he was seized with fever. He began with having pain in the loins; he had heaviness of the head, and there was stiffness of the neck. On the first day . . . he was thirsty, tongue dry; no sleep at night. On the second, acute fever . . . an uncomfortable night, slight delirium. . . . On the sixth, slight perspiration about the head . . . much tossing about; no passage from the bowels, urine suppressed, acute fever. On the seventh, loss of speech; extremities [hands and feet] could no longer be kept warm; no discharge of urine."

Hippocrates also noted that the patient died on the eleventh day. Hippocrates and other ancient Greek doctors did not know enough about the workings of the human body to treat serious illnesses. They did not know about germs or how germs cause disease. They did not know how to keep wounds from becoming infected. They did not know much about the workings of the heart, the lungs, and other organs. Although Hippocrates took a scientific approach to medicine, his medical knowledge was very limited. He treated patients with plant remedies, wound dressings, and minor surgery. But he could not save everyone.

HIPPOCRATES' OATH

Legend says that Hippocrates made his students take a pledge. They had to promise to practice medicine in an ethical way. In fact, many ancient Greek doctors did take such an oath. We call it the Hippocratic oath, although Hippocrates probably didn't write it.

In the oath, ancient Greek doctors swore to use medicine for good and not for harm. They promised never to give a poisonous drug to a patient. They also promised to respect patients' privacy. Modern doctors take a similar oath.

> "I swear by Apollo the physician, and by Asklepios, Hygeia and Panacea, and all the gods and goddesses, and call them to witness that . . . I will prescribe treatments to the best of my ability and judgment for the good of the sick, and never for a harmful or illicit [unlawful] purpose."

—Hippocratic oath excerpt, circa 500s B.C.

THE FIRST SHRINK

People in the ancient world did not know much about mental illness. Many groups thought that witches or evil spirits caused mental illness. Some societies locked up mentally ill people and treated them cruelly. In ancient Greece, some doctors recommended that mentally ill patients be kept in dark rooms. They thought darkness had a soothing effect on troubled minds.

Around 100 B.C., a Greek physician named Asclepiades (above) took a new approach to mental illness. He urged that mentally ill people be treated humanely. He treated them with special diets and warm baths. He even used music to calm disturbed patients. Asclepiades realized that some mentally ill people had hallucinations (imaginary visions) in the dark. So he moved them into well-lit rooms.

Asclepiades was ahead of his time. In the following centuries, physicians did not show as much compassion toward the mentally ill as he had. It wasn't until the twentieth century that doctors again embraced humane treatment of the mentally ill.

THE FOUR HUMORS

Like the ancient Chinese, the ancient Greeks thought that sickness resulted when the body was out of balance. Greek physicians thought that four humors, or fluids, controlled human health. These humors were phlegm, blood, yellow bile, and black bile. The fluids were part of a larger philosophy, or belief system. In this philosophy, each of the four humors was associated with a different natural substance, a specific moisture and temperature, a certain part of the body, and a certain season of the year. The associations were as follows:

HUMOR	NATURAL SUBSTANCE	MOISTURE AND TEMPERATURE	BODY PART	SEASON
Phlegm	Water	Wet and cold	Brain	Winter
Blood	Air	Wet and hot	Blood	Spring
Yellow bile	Fire	Dry and hot	Liver	Summer
Black bile	Earth	Dry and cold	Spleen	Autumn

In *Airs, Waters, and Places*, which is part of the Hippocratic Collection, the writer explains these connections further:

> A city that is exposed to hot winds ... but which is sheltered from the north winds; in such a city the waters will be plenteous and saltish, and as they run from an elevated source, they are necessarily hot in summer, and cold in winter; the heads of the inhabitants are of a humid ... constitution, and their bellies subject to frequent disorders, owing to the phlegm running down from the head. ... The women are sickly and subject to excessive menstruation; then many are unfruitful from disease, and not from nature, and they have frequent miscarriages; infants are subject to attacks of convulsions and asthma, which they consider to be connected with infancy, and hold to be a sacred disease [epilepsy]. The men are subject to attacks of dysentery, diarrhea ... chronic fevers in winter.

With such guidelines in mind, it was the ancient Greek physician's job to balance the humors. Suppose a patient had a fever. His or her body was hot and dry. So the physician believed the patient had too much yellow bile. The physician would try to restore balance by increasing the patient's phlegm, which was wet and cold—the opposite of hot and dry. The physician might prescribe a cold bath.

Often ancient Greek physicians tried to rid patients of excessive humors. Physicians cut and bled patients to rid them of too much blood. They often prescribed medicine made of hellebore, a poisonous plant. The medicine caused any number of severe reactions, including sneezing, vomiting, diarrhea, and muscle cramps. Ancient Greek physicians thought these reactions were beneficial. Through vomiting or diarrhea, physicians thought, patients would rid themselves of the excess humors that made them sick. In fact, hellebore actually just made patients sicker. In some cases, it even killed them.

"TO CUT UP"

Our modern medical term *anatomy* comes from ancient Greek words that mean "to cut up." The study of human anatomy involves dissecting, or cutting up, dead bodies. Anatomy is one of the first courses medical students take. Doctors must know how the body is put together to diagnose and treat diseases.

The ancient Greeks laid the basis for this key area of medical science. In the 500s B.C., a man named Alcmaeon was the first person to dissect human bodies for scientific study. He wrote descriptions of the optic nerve in the human eye and the eustachian tube inside the ear.

The Greek physician Herophilus (ca. 335–280 B.C.) was another anatomy pioneer. He started a medical school in Alexandria, Egypt. Although not officially part of Greece, this city was home to many ancient Greek scholars and scientists. At Alexandria, Herophilus wrote the first detailed description of the human brain. He recognized the brain as the seat of intelligence. He described differences between two key parts of the brain, the cerebrum and cerebellum. He suggested that nerves are involved in the senses. He also recognized the difference between arteries, which carry fresh, oxygen-rich blood away from the heart, and veins, which carry blood from body tissues back to the heart.

MEDICAL MATTER

In the first century A.D., a Greek physician named Pedanius Dioscorides wrote one of the most complete descriptions of ancient medicinal plants. His book was called *De Materia Medica (left)*, which means "concerning medical matter." The book described about five hundred medicinal plants. It included illustrations of many of them. It was the most respected book on drugs in the world for almost twelve hundred years. But modern doctors who have studied the book say that only about 20 percent of the plants would actually have helped patients.

An anatomist named Erasistratos worked with Herophilus at Alexandria. According to Aulus Cornelius Celsus, a Roman writer, the two men even performed dissections on *living* people. Celsus wrote:

> Herophilus and Erasistratos . . . laid open men whilst [while] alive—criminals received out of prison from the kings—and whilst these were still breathing, observed parts of which beforehand nature had concealed, their position, [color], shape, size, arrangement, hardness, softness, smoothness, relation, processes and depressions of each, and whether any part is inserted into or received into another.

Celsus, who lived several centuries after Herophilus and Erasistratos, condemned their experiments as cruel. He said that surgeons could look inside the bodies of people who were already severely wounded, such as

These pictures were carved on the wall of a temple built to honor Asclepius, the Greek god of healing. Scalpels are shown in the center. The objects on each side of the scalpels are cupping glasses. Ancient doctors used the glasses to draw blood from the body.

accident victims and gladiators (professional warriors), instead of cutting up people on purpose.

As cruel as the experiments were, they helped improve ancient Greek medical knowledge. By studying anatomy, ancient Greek surgeons learned to do major surgery. They learned how to safely amputate limbs, repair hernias, and remove stones from the bladder.

THE PUS PULLER

Few medical devices are more important than the syringe. Doctors and nurses use syringes to inject medicine, take blood samples, and drain fluid from the body. Early peoples in many cultures made syringes out of hollow bones and animal bladders. The ancient Greeks used similar devices made from animal bladders and thin metal pipes. They used these devices to squirt air or liquid onto wounds or into body cavities.

Ctesibius, a Greek engineer from Alexandria, invented a new kind of syringe around 280 B.C. This syringe was made of two pieces of metal: a piston, or sliding valve, and a hollow cylinder. The cylinder tapered to a point at one end. Pushing on the piston forced air or liquid inside the cylinder to squirt out at the pointed end. Drawing back on the piston sucked material from wounds or body cavities. The first description of the cylinder-and-piston syringe appears in a book called *Pneumatics*. It was written by Hero of Alexandria in the first century A.D.

The ancient Greeks used syringes mostly to suck pus out of pimples, boils, and infected wounds. The Greek name for the syringe, *pyulkos*, means "pus puller."

CHAPTER SEVEN

ANCIENT ROME

Ancient Rome began as a small city around 900 B.C. Over the following centuries, the ancient Romans built a great empire. It was based in modern–day Italy. By the first century A.D., the empire reached all the way to central Europe, the Middle East, and northern Africa.

The Romans conquered other countries and adopted foreign technology, including medical technology. Rome borrowed much medical and other technology from ancient Greece. According to one ancient writer, Rome was "swept along on the puffs of the clever brains of Greece."

Historians think the Romans also adopted Indian medical technology. The ancient Romans and ancient Indians often traded with each other. The Romans loved pepper on their food. They imported pepper and other spices from India. Roman traders also brought back medicines and information about surgical procedures from India. One Roman historian complained that people ignored medicinal plants growing around their own country because so many effective medicines came from India.

ON MEDICINE

Aulus Cornelius Celsus was a wealthy Roman landowner. He lived during the first century A.D. Celsus wrote a

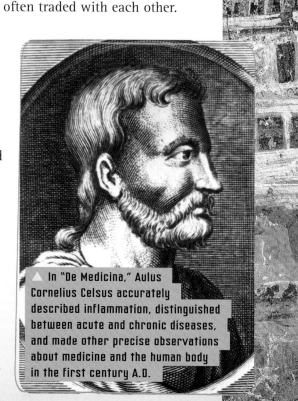

▲ In "De Medicina," Aulus Cornelius Celsus accurately described inflammation, distinguished between acute and chronic diseases, and made other precise observations about medicine and the human body in the first century A.D.

long book on warfare, farming, medicine, science, law, and philosophy. The medical chapter was called "De Medicina," or "On Medicine." The chapter was divided into eight sections. They described diseases, treatments, special diets, surgery, and other medical topics.

▼ The Romans took advantage of medical technology developed in other empires. This fresco shows the ancient Italian port of Stabiae, where merchants unloaded ships full of medicines and other goods from India. This art is now at a museum in Naples, Italy.

"De Medicina" provided accurate descriptions of many medical terms. For instance, doctors around the world still use Celsus's definition of inflammation. Celsus said there were four basic signs of inflammation. They were "rubor et tumor cum calore et dolore." This Latin phrase translates as "redness and swelling with heat and pain."

Modern doctors recognize two basic kinds of disease: chronic and acute. Chronic diseases, such as arthritis, last a long time. Patients may live with them for decades. Acute diseases, such as infections, end quickly. The end may be good or bad. The patient may recover quickly or die quickly. Celsus left modern medicine with a precise definition of acute diseases. He wrote: "Qui cito vel tollunt hominem, vel ipsi cito finiuntur." The English translation is: "[The diseases] either finish the man quickly, or finish themselves quickly."

TO CUT UP, CONTINUED

The ancient study of anatomy that began with Herophilus in Greece reached a peak with Galen in Rome. Galen was born in Pergamum (in modern day Turkey) in A.D. 129. At the time, Pergamum was part of the Roman Empire. Galen studied medicine in Alexandria. Then he returned to Pergamum. There, he learned a great deal about wounds and the insides of the human body by treating wounded gladiators.

In A.D. 162, Galen moved to the city of Rome. He became the physician to Emperor Marcus Aurelius and his family. Along with this job, Galen continued his own medical research and writing. He learned more about the human body by dissecting monkeys. Since monkeys and humans evolved from the same animal ancestors, their bodies are similar. Galen also studied human skeletons.

Galen studied other animals too. In one experiment, he operated on a pig. He wanted to determine whether a nerve in the pig's neck controlled its breathing. He cut the nerve, and the pig kept breathing. But it was

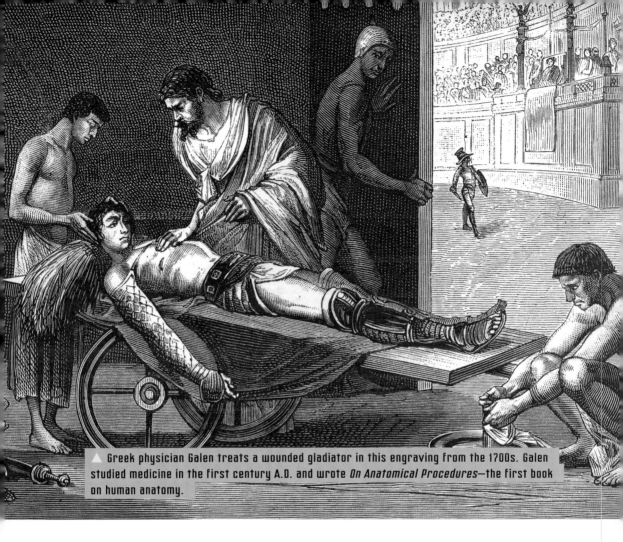

▲ Greek physician Galen treats a wounded gladiator in this engraving from the 1700s. Galen studied medicine in the first century A.D. and wrote *On Anatomical Procedures*—the first book on human anatomy.

unable to squeal. So Galen realized that a comparable nerve in humans, the recurrent laryngeal nerve, controls speech. This information helped other physicians when they operated on the human thyroid, a gland in the front of the neck. They knew to avoid cutting the recurrent laryngeal nerve. If the nerve were accidentally cut, patients sometimes could not speak afterward. The recurrent laryngeal nerve is still also called Galen's nerve.

Galen put all his knowledge into a sixteen-volume book called *On Anatomical Procedures*. It is considered the first textbook on human anatomy.

GALEN'S LEGACY

Greek physician Galen *(right)* wrote about more than five hundred medicines derived from plants. He often mixed plant medicines together in complicated prescriptions. Some mixtures contained dozens of ingredients. In modern times, physicians use the term *galenical preparations* to describe drugs made from plants.

TAKING YOUR PULSE

As part of a medical examination, Galen would take a patient's pulse. The pulse is the rhythmic expansion and contraction of a person's arteries. Doctors often feel a patient's pulse in his or her wrist. The pulse mirrors the pumping action of the person's heart. If the pulse is too fast, too slow, or irregular, it may indicate heart disease. In an essay called "On the Pulse," Galen wrote:

> The heart and all the arteries pulsate with the same rhythm, so that from one you can judge of all. . . . But you could not find any arteries more convenient or more suitable for taking the pulse than those in the wrists, for they are easily visible, as there is little flesh over them, and it is not necessary to strip away any part of the body of clothing for them, as is necessary with many others, and they run in a straight course; and this is of no small help in the accuracy of diagnosis.

The Roman emperor Julius Caesar has been falsely linked with the cesarean section, a surgical method of delivering a baby. Caesar himself was probably born through a nonsurgical birth in 100 B.C.

THE CESAREAN SECTION

In human birth, a newborn comes into the world through his or her mother's birth canal. But in some cases, the baby cannot pass through the birth canal safely. So doctors must perform a cesarean section. In this surgery, doctors make an incision into the mother's abdomen and uterus to remove the baby.

Many people think the term *cesarean* originated from the surgical birth of Julius Caesar. He was Rome's emperor from 48 to 44 B.C. But medical historians think that Caesar probably was not born by cesarean section. At the time of Caesar's birth, Roman doctors performed the operation only when the mother was dying or dead and therefore could not push the baby out herself. But Julius Caesar's mother was alive long after his birth. So she probably gave birth to him through her birth canal. The word *cesarean* may actually come from another Latin word, *caedare*, which means "to cut open."

Cesarean sections were probably performed long before Roman times. Ancient Indian and Egyptian writings mention surgical births. One ancient Chinese picture shows the operation.

ANCIENT OB-GYN

Female doctors were common in ancient Rome. Most of them focused on diseases specific to women. A *medica a mammis* was a female doctor who specialized in breast health. *Obstetrices* were midwives. They cared for pregnant women and delivered babies.

ANCIENT EYE SURGERY

Mention eye surgery and people usually think of lasers and other high-tech equipment. Most people don't know that ancient doctors performed eye surgery more than two thousand years ago. It was cataract surgery, an operation to remove a clouded lens from the eye.

Ancient Indian surgeons probably invented cataract surgery. Sushruta wrote a long description of the technique. Celsus described a technique very similar to Sushruta's. In fact, the techniques are so similar that historians think the Romans learned about the technology from Indian doctors or from Indian medical books.

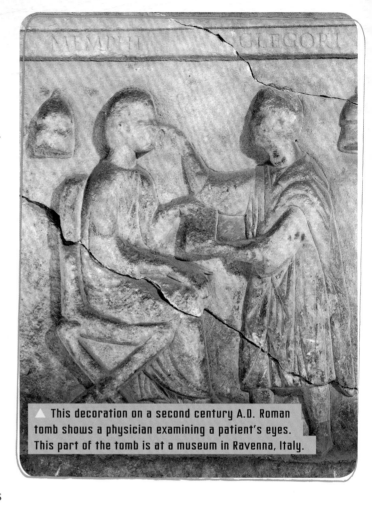

▲ This decoration on a second century A.D. Roman tomb shows a physician examining a patient's eyes. This part of the tomb is at a museum in Ravenna, Italy.

Ancient doctors performed the surgery with a fine needle. They inserted the needle into a patient's eye. They carefully pushed the clouded lens to the bottom of the eyeball. Celsus knew the danger of this procedure. If the needle slipped and touched the retina, the tissue-thin membrane at the back of the eye, the patient would go blind. Celsus advised other doctors to tie down the patient or to have a strong assistant hold the patient still, so that he or she didn't move during the operation. Celsus explained that the surgeon's needle should be:

inserted at a spot between the pupil of the eye and the angle adjacent to the temple, away from the middle of the cataract, in such a way that no vein is wounded. When the spot is reached, the needle is to be sloped against the lens itself and rotated gently, guiding it little by little below the pupil. When the cataract has passed below the pupil, it is pressed upon more firmly in order that it may settle below. After this the needle is drawn straight out; and soft wool soaked in white of egg is to be put on, and above this something to check inflammation; and then a bandage.

When modern doctors perform cataract surgery, they remove the clouded lens from the eye and replace it with an artificial lens. Sometimes cataract patients must wear contact lenses or eyeglasses after the surgery to see clearly. Ancient doctors did not replace clouded lenses with artificial lenses. Ancient peoples also did not have eyeglasses or contact lenses. So a patient's vision would have been badly blurred after cataract surgery in ancient times. But the patient would still have seen better than he or she did without the surgery.

> "[In swamps] are bred certain minute [tiny] creatures which cannot be seen by the eyes, which float through the air and enter the body through the mouth and the nose and there cause serious disease."
>
> —Marcus Terentius Varro, Roman scholar, first century B.C.

PRESERVED IN ASH

Archaeologists have found hundreds of ancient Roman surgical instruments. These instruments were made with great precision. For example, Roman forceps were high-quality metal tools. Their jaws aligned precisely and closed tightly when grasping. Medical historians note that Roman surgical instruments were much better than the instruments available to surgeons during the Renaissance, which began in Europe in the 1300s, more than one thousand years later.

Archaeologists have found many surgical instruments in the remains of Pompeii. This ancient Roman city was destroyed when Mount Vesuvius, a

▼ These surgical instruments—including forceps, clamps, and drills—were used in the ancient Roman city of Pompeii. A volcanic eruption destroyed the city in A.D. 79.

volcano, erupted in A.D. 79. The eruption rained poisonous gases, cinders, and hot ashes down on the city. Some buildings fell to the ground during the eruption. The hot ashes and poisonous gases killed many of the city's residents. The ash later cooled and hardened around people's bodies and other objects. Archaeologists have found ancient Roman medical kits preserved inside hardened shells of ash. The kits consisted of hollow, pocket-sized metal cylinders with probes, scalpels, and other medical tools inside.

ROMAN BARB PULLER

Warfare in ancient Rome was just as bloody and murderous as it is in modern times. Soldiers killed one another with spears and arrows. Some spearheads and arrowheads had barbs, or extra points that projected backward. Barbed points were difficult to remove from the body. Pulling them out usually caused more damage, because the barbs caught on tissue and tore it.

Roman doctors used a clever device to pull barbed arrowheads and spearheads from wounded patients. It was a spoonlike instrument shaped like a shoehorn. A doctor inserted the device behind an arrowhead or spearhead and caught the main point in a hole in the bowl of the spoon. The spoon formed a shield around the barb. The doctor could then remove the object without causing further damage.

SANITATION

Many of Rome's most important advances in medical technology did not involve the treatment of disease. They involved disease prevention through sanitation and public health measures. The term *sanitation* means "the removal of wastewater to promote health and cleanliness." *Public health* refers to government efforts to keep everyone in a city or community healthy. One of the most important public health measures in ancient Rome was sewage disposal.

Every street in the city of Rome had a sewer running along its length. The homes of wealthy people had indoor toilets. Pipes carried human waste directly from these toilets into city sewers. Less wealthy people used chamber pots as toilets. They emptied waste from the pots into sewers themselves. Rome even had public toilets located along the sewers. People could use the toilets when they were away from home.

Water flowed continuously through each sewer. The water emptied into larger and larger channels. Eventually, all the sewers in Rome emptied into the Cloaca Maxima, or "Big Sewer." The Cloaca Maxima emptied into the Tiber River.

PURE WATER

Rome's sewer system had one big drawback. Sewage emptying into the Tiber River polluted the water. Thousands of people got sick from drinking polluted river water. People in ancient Rome needed a source of clean drinking water.

Rome solved the problem by building its famous aqueduct system. The word *aqueduct* means "water channel" in Latin. Aqueducts carried clean water from mountain springs

▲ The ancient Romans built public toilets in Rome and other parts of their empire. These toilets were in a Roman colony in modern-day Libya in northern Africa.

Aqueducts such as this one in Merida, Spain, once brought clean mountain water to cities of the Roman Empire. Clean drinking water helped keep ancient Romans healthy.

in the countryside into the city of Rome. Some aqueducts were elevated. They looked like tall bridges. Other aqueducts were underground channels. All Roman aqueducts were built with a slight slope, so that water flowed downward into the city. That way, engineers didn't have to equip the channels with pumps to move the water.

The Roman leader Appius Claudius ordered the building of Rome's first aqueduct in 312 B.C. It was 11 miles (17 kilometers) long and ran almost entirely underground. Eventually, engineers built ten more aqueducts for Rome. The aqueducts brought almost 85 million gallons (322 million liters) of water into the city each day. Engineers built more aqueducts in other parts of the Roman Empire.

This aerial photograph shows Housesteads Roman Fort in northern Britain. Romans built the fort around A.D. 124. One of the fort buildings was a *valetudinaria*, or hospital.

THE HOSPITAL SYSTEM

At its height, the Roman Empire controlled a vast territory. The empire stretched from central Europe to northern Africa to the Middle East. Roman legions, or military divisions, fought battles far from home. When a Roman soldier was wounded, he had to be treated quickly, on-site. So the Roman military built special clinics at military camps. The buildings were called valetudinaria. The name means "places of health" in Latin. They were the first permanent hospitals.

Archaeologists have discovered the ruins of at least twenty–five valetudinaria in the former Roman Empire. Most were built during the A.D. 100s and 200s. The builders followed a standard plan. In each hospital, small wards opened off a central corridor. Each ward usually held four patients. Each ward also had a work area where staff prepared medicines and food for patients.

Archaeologists have found the remains of medicines and medical instruments in the ruins of some valetudinaria. In one, archaeologists found seeds of the henbane plant. This plant contains the drug scopolamine. Modern doctors use scopolamine to treat nausea and motion sickness. The drug can also make people drowsy. Roman physicians combined scopolamine with opium. This combination made patients drowsy and relieved their pain.

EPILOGUE

AFTER THE ANCIENTS

▲ When the plague struck Europe in the mid-1300s, doctors were nearly powerless to help the sick. Doctors of this era didn't know about the bacterium that causes plague, and they had no antibiotics.

Ancient societies rose and fell. Often groups grew politically or economically weak, and stronger groups conquered them. But even after a culture died out, its technology often remained. Conquering groups built on the knowledge of conquered peoples to further develop technology.

This wasn't always the case, however. After the Roman Empire fell to invaders in A.D. 476, Europe entered a period called the Middle Ages (about 500 to 1500). The early Middle Ages are sometimes called the Dark Ages

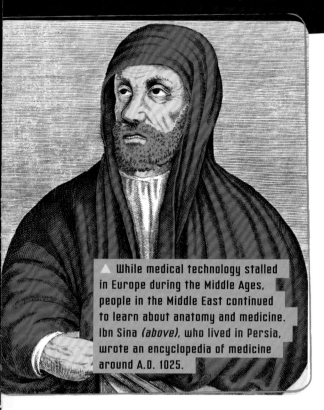

▲ While medical technology stalled in Europe during the Middle Ages, people in the Middle East continued to learn about anatomy and medicine. Ibn Sina *(above)*, who lived in Persia, wrote an encyclopedia of medicine around A.D. 1025.

because art, culture, and learning were minimal in Europe during these years. Few people in Europe went to school. Few craftspeople knew about or improved upon ancient technology.

Europeans made few advances in medicine during the Middle Ages. Some religious groups operated hospitals. Medical schools opened in some European cities. But for the most part, European doctors didn't improve upon the medical knowledge of the ancient Greeks and Romans. In fact, a lot of that knowledge was lost. Many libraries were neglected during the Middle Ages. Some libraries burned to the ground. Others were destroyed in war. In this way, many writings about ancient medicine disappeared.

At the same time, people forgot about the public health measures used by the ancient Romans. In some European cities, people dumped human and animal wastes right into city streets. They drank water from polluted rivers. Unsanitary conditions led to many outbreaks of disease.

The medical situation was better in the Middle East during the Middle Ages. Physicians there carried on with the study of medicine begun by the ancient Greeks. Middle Eastern doctors operated medical schools, studied anatomy, and improved surgical techniques. In the Persian Empire (based in modern-day Iran), a doctor named Ibn Sina (A.D. 980–1037) compiled a medical encyclopedia. Called the *Canon of Medicine*, it was the most advanced medical book of the Middle Ages. It contained descriptions of diseases, medicines, anatomy, physiology, and psychology.

DEATH AND REBIRTH

In the 1300s, an epidemic of plague swept through Europe. Infected people got fevers, headaches, body aches, and painful swellings on parts of their bodies. They usually died within five days of infection. Some people thought the plague was a punishment from God. They didn't know that plague was caused by bacteria. They didn't understand how it spread from person to person. Physicians tried all sorts of remedies, but they were nearly powerless to help people who got sick with plague. By the time the epidemic ended, the "Black Death" had killed one-quarter to one-half of Europe's people.

On the heels of the Black Death, Europe entered an era called the Renaissance (early 1300s–1600). *Renaissance* means "rebirth." The era was a time of great artistic, scientific, and intellectual achievement in Europe. During this period, Europeans rediscovered some of the technology and knowledge of ancient Greece and Rome. European doctors once again began to study human anatomy, diseases, and medicines.

Italian scholars found an ancient copy of Celsus's "De Medicina" in the early 1400s. Soon afterward, a German man named Johannes Gutenberg invented the printing press. This machine enabled people to print many copies of a book in a short time. In 1478 scholars reprinted "De Medicina." It was the first medical book reproduced on the printing press.

Renaissance scholars were excited to discover an ancient copy of "De Medicina." They reprinted the ancient Greek medical book using the newly invented printing press. The printed book's index is shown below.

THE FLOODGATES OF KNOWLEDGE

In the 1500s, European medical knowledge began to surpass the knowledge of ancient Greece and Rome. Italian artist and inventor Leonardo da Vinci performed dissections and made drawings of the body parts he saw. A French doctor named Ambroise Paré studied gunshot wounds and surgical wounds. He determined that wounds healed best when left to heal naturally. He advised against using cautery. In the early 1600s, English physician William Harvey studied the human circulatory system—the way blood travels throughout the body. He learned about the workings of the heart, the arteries, and the veins. In the late 1700s, British physician Edward Jenner discovered a new way to protect people from smallpox. His procedure, called vaccination, was safer than the ancient Indian practice of variolation.

▲ Vaccination, a smallpox-prevention technique devised by British doctor Edward Jenner in 1796, was safer than variolation. This nineteenth-century painting shows Jenner vaccinating a child. In modern times, vaccination is used to protect people from a variety of diseases.

More breakthroughs followed. In the 1800s, doctors learned how to anesthetize parts of the body, or deaden them to pain, before surgery. Using microscopes, doctors identified bacteria and viruses that can cause disease. They devised more vaccinations to prevent more diseases. They discovered how to look inside the body using X–rays.

Around the turn of the twentieth century, governments enacted new public health measures. Big cities in Europe, the United States, and other places installed water and sewage systems. These systems ensured that people had clean water to drink and that wastewater was carried away safely. Public health nurses vaccinated children against diseases and taught them about good hygiene, or personal cleanliness.

A dramatic medical breakthrough occurred in 1928. That year doctors discovered antibiotics. These are medicines that kill bacteria. These "wonder drugs" cure many diseases and keep wounds from becoming infected. The

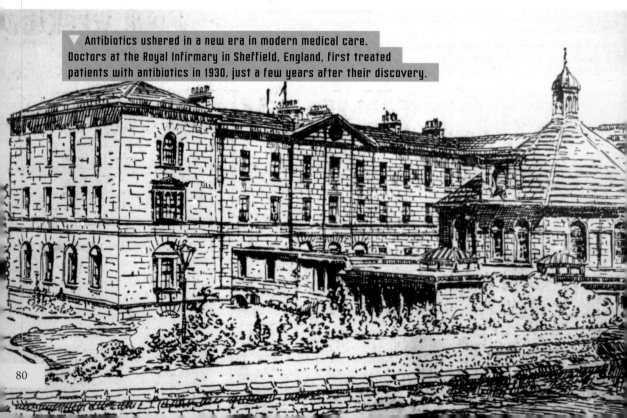

▼ Antibiotics ushered in a new era in modern medical care. Doctors at the Royal Infirmary in Sheffield, England, first treated patients with antibiotics in 1930, just a few years after their discovery.

discovery of antibiotics ushered in a new era of health care. Doctors used antibiotics to treat people with meningitis, tuberculosis, scarlet fever, and other diseases. Before antibiotics, these diseases were often fatal. After antibiotics, people who got these diseases were usually cured.

THE GOOD OLD DAYS

By the late twentieth century, medicine was high-tech and highly effective, especially in wealthy nations such as the United States. People laughed and sometimes shuddered when they thought about ancient treatments such as bloodletting and cautery. They snickered at old ideas and thought that ancient medicine was barbaric.

But not everyone was laughing. In some places, people hadn't discarded ancient healing methods entirely. For instance, people in China still practiced acupuncture in the twentieth century. In 1972 U.S. president Richard Nixon made a trip to China to improve ties between that country and the United States. As part of the visit, Nixon and other Americans watched an acupuncture demonstration. The Americans were amazed. They saw Chinese doctors using acupuncture as anesthesia before surgery. In other words, acupuncture deadened sensation in parts of patients' bodies. The patients felt no pain during surgery.

Back in the United States, some people began studying acupuncture. They realized that it was effective for treating some injuries and ailments. U.S. acupuncturists used diagrams of the human body created by ancient Chinese physicians. They learned about yin and yang and the body's fourteen major meridians. They learned that inserting a needle in one part of the body could treat an ailment in another part. For instance, inserting a needle into a certain part of a patient's hand might alleviate his or her headaches.

In 1996 the U.S. Food and Drug Administration, the government agency that oversees U.S. medical treatments, devices, and drugs, announced that acupuncture was safe and effective for treating some ailments. Since then,

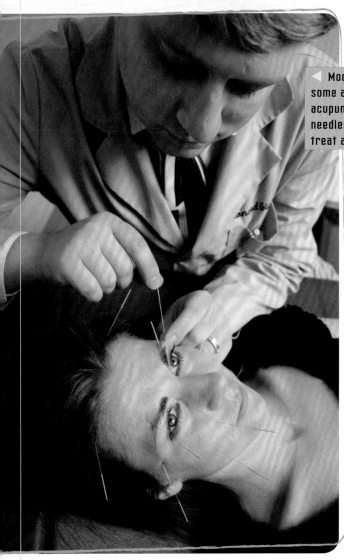

acupuncture has grown in popularity in the United States and elsewhere. Acupuncture schools have opened across the United States. Many doctors trained in Western (European–based) medicine have teamed up with acupuncturists to treat patients. Some acupuncturists work independently.

Acupuncture was just the beginning. Some Americans began studying the ayurvedic medicine of ancient India. Others explored ancient Native American healing practices. Many learned about the medicinal herbs of ancient China. Modern people realized that ancient cultures were anything but backward and barbaric when it came to medicine. Many of their remedies really worked—and still do.

In the 400s B.C., ancient Greek doctors prescribed the leaves and bark of the willow tree for pain. Modern doctors know that willow leaves and bark contain a chemical called salicin. Once inside the human body, salicin turns into salicylate. Salicylate is the main ingredient in aspirin, one of the most common pain relievers in the modern world. The ancient Greeks couldn't go

▲ Many people use ancient Chinese medicines as a complement to Western medicine. At this store in Vancouver, British Columbia, Canada, people can buy traditional Chinese plant remedies.

to the drugstore and buy a jar of aspirin. But they didn't need to. They could simply go to a riverbank, collect some willow branches, head home, and brew some willow tea.

Ancient medicine certainly wasn't superior or even close in quality to modern medicine. But ancient people devised effective medical technology with the materials at hand. They came up with practical solutions to health problems. Their solutions were limited because their knowledge of human health was limited. But sometimes their solutions were lifesavers.

TIMELINE

2600s B.C.	Imhotep practices medicine in ancient Egypt.
CA. 2500 B.C.	Peseshet, a female doctor, practices medicine in ancient Egypt.
CA. 1900 B.C.	Ancient Egyptians write about medicine in the Kahun Papyrus.
CA. 1600 B.C.	Ancient Egyptians write about medicine in the Edwin Smith Papyrus.
CA. 1500 B.C.	Ancient Egyptians write about medicine in the Ebers Papyrus.
CA. 600 B.C.	Tarquinius Priscus begins building Rome's sewer system.
500s B.C.	Alcmaeon of Croton is the first person to dissect human bodies for medical study.
430-425 B.C.	The Great Plague of Athens strikes Greece. It kills one-third to one-half of the Greek population.
400s B.C.	Hippocrates teaches medicine on the island of Cos. Greek doctors write the Hippocratic Collection.
400s OR 300s B.C.	Ancient Chinese write down the *Nei Ching*.
312 B.C.	Appius Claudius orders the building of Rome's first aqueduct.
300s B.C.	Herophilus founds a medical school in Alexandria, Egypt.
CA. 280 B.C.	Ctesibius of Alexandria invents a cylinder-and-piston syringe.
CA. 100 B.C.	Asclepiades advocates for humane treatments for the mentally ill.
CA. A.D. 40-90	Pedanius Dioscorides writes *De Materia Medica*. Aulus Cornelius Celsus writes "De Medicina."
	The Indian surgeon Sushruta writes the *Sushruta Samhita*.
100s	Galen practices and studies medicine in Rome. Roman armies build *valetudinaria* (hospitals) at military camps.
542	Plague strikes Turkey, killing almost half the population of Constantinople (Istanbul).
1300s	Plague kills up to one-half of Europe's people.
1478	Italian scholars reprint Celsus's "De Medicina."

1500s	European explorers bring new diseases to the Americas.
1867	French physician Paul Broca discovers that ancient people performed trepanation (cutting or drilling a hole in the skull).
1972	President Richard Nixon and other Americans witness an acupuncture demonstration in China.
1996	U.S. scientists propose that Ebola virus caused the Great Plague of Athens. The U.S. Food and Drug Administration says that acupuncture is safe and effective for treating some ailments.
2003	Laborers discover the bodies of Oldcroghan Man and Clonycavan Man in peat bogs in Ireland.
2006	Greek scientists propose that typhoid fever caused the Great Plague of Athens.
2010	Scientists discover that Egypt's King Tut probably died from malaria.

GLOSSARY

ABSCESS: a collection of pus surrounded by inflamed tissue

ACUPUNCTURE: a Chinese practice of inserting fine needles into the skin along the body's meridians (energy pathways) to cure disease or relieve pain

ANESTHETIC: a medicine that reduces or eliminates the sensation of pain

ANTIBIOTIC: a medicine, such as penicillin, that kills or slows the growth of bacteria

ANTISEPTIC: a substance that prevents or slows the growth of germs

ARCHAEOLOGIST: a scientist who studies the remains of past human cultures

BACTERIA: microscopic single-cell organisms. Some bacteria cause disease.

BLEEDING: letting blood out of the body in an effort to cure sickness

CATARACT: a clouding of the lens of the eye

CAUTERY: burning the skin in an effort to stop bleeding or to heal a wound

DISSECTION: cutting apart an animal or a plant to study its internal structure

EPIDEMIC: an outbreak of disease that affects a large number of people in the same region at the same time

FORCEPS: tweezerlike tools used by physicians and dentists for grasping or holding or pulling at parts of the body

GYNECOLOGY: the branch of medicine that deals with functions and diseases of the female reproductive system

HUMAN ANATOMY: the structure of the human body, including the skeleton, muscles, nerves, and organs

IMMUNITY: built-in resistance to a particular disease

INCISION: a cut made into the body

INFLAMMATION: a response by the body to injury or infection. Inflammation causes redness, swelling, heat, and pain.

MUMMY: a dead body that has been preserved by either humans or environmental conditions

PLAGUE: a disease caused by the bacterium *Yersinia pestis.* The term can also refer to any widespread outbreak of deadly disease.

PLASTER: a cloth treated with medicine and applied to a wound or an injury; also called a poultice

PLASTIC SURGERY: repairing or replacing deformed, damaged, or lost body parts to improve their appearance or function

POULTICE: a cloth treated with medicine and applied to a wound or an injury; also called a plaster

PUBLIC HEALTH: government or community efforts to maintain and improve people's health. Examples include vaccination and sanitation.

SANITATION: the cleaning or disposing of waterborne waste within a community to promote health

SHAMAN: a priest or priestess who uses magic and other techniques to cure the sick, tell the future, and communicate with spirits

SYRINGE: a device used to inject fluids into or withdraw fluids from the body

TREPANATION: a surgical operation in which a circular piece of bone is cut from the skull to expose the brain

VACCINATION: an injection that protects people from disease. Most vaccinations contain killed or weakened bacteria or viruses.

VARIOLATION: an ancient method of giving someone a weakened form of smallpox to make the person immune to smallpox afterward

SOURCE NOTES

12 *Old Celtic Romances*, P. W. Joyce, trans., (New York: MacMillan and Company, 1894), 92.

17 Guido Majno, *The Healing Hand: Man and Wound in the Ancient World* (Cambridge, MA: Harvard University Press, 1991), 73.

18 Christos Evangeliou, *Hellenic Philosophy: Origin and Character* (Aldershot, UK: Ashgate Publishing, 2006), 12.

18 Michael J. O'Dowd, *The History of Medications for Women* (New York: Parthenon Publishing, 2001), 49.

20 James Henry Breasted, ed., *The Edwin Smith Surgical Papyrus* (Chicago: University of Chicago, 1930), 266.

27–28 "An English Translation of the Sushruta Samhita," Internet Archive, n.d., http://www.archive.org/stream/englishtranslati00susruoft/englishtranslati00susruoft_djvu.txt (July 12, 2010).

28 Ibid.

29 Majno, *Healing Hand*, 285.

30 Ibid., 291.

31 "Sushruta Samhita," Internet Archive.

36 Paul Ulrich Unschuld, *Medical Ethics in Imperial China: A Study in Historical Anthropology* (Berkeley: University of Californa Press, 1979), 39.

38 Ilza Veith, ed. and trans., *Huang Ti Nei Ching Su Wen: The Yellow Emperor's Classic of Internal Medicine* (Berkeley: University of California Press, 1973), 50.

40 Song Wan and Anthony P. C. Yim, *Cardiothoracic Surgery in China: Past, Present and Future* (Hong Kong: Chinese University Press, 2007), 210.

41 Majno, *Healing Hand*, 237.

44 Virgil J. Vogel, *American Indian Medicine* (Norman: University of Oklahoma Press, 1970), 181–182.

46 Ibid., 54.

51 Gerald David Hart, *Asclepius: The God of Medicine* (London: Royal Medical Press, 2000), 69.

52 Thucydides, "The History of the Peloponnesian War," available online at Project Gutenberg, May 1, 2009, http://www.gutenberg.org/files/7142/7142.txt (July 12, 2010).

54 "Greek Texts and Translations," Perseus Digital Library at Tufts, July 2009, http://perseus.uchicago.edu/perseus-cgi/citequery3.pl?dbname=GreekTexts&getid=1&query=Hipp.%20Epid.%201.4.4 (July 12, 2010).

55 Jenny Sutcliffe and Nancy Duin, *A History of Medicine* (New York: Barnes and Nobles Books, 1992), 18.

57 Hippocrates, "On Airs, Waters, and Places," available online at Internet Classics Archive, 2009, http://classics.mit.edu/Hippocrates/airwatpl.3.3.html (July 12, 2010).

59 Aulus Cornelius Celsus, "De Medicina," available online at Bill Thayer's Web Site, July 11, 2010, http://penelope.uchicago.edu/Thayer/E/Roman/Texts/Celsus/Prooemium*.html (July 12, 2010).

62 Majno, *Healing Hand*, 341.

64 Sutcliffe and Duin, *History of Medicine*, 21.

64 Aulus Cornelius Celsus, *On Medicine* (London: E. Cox, 1831), 145.

66 Logan Clendening, *Source Book of Medical History* (Toronto: General Publishing Company, 1942), 42.

69 Peter James and Nick Thorpe, *Ancient Inventions* (New York: Ballantine Books, 1994), 19.

69 Sutcliffe and Duin, *History of Medicine*, 21.

SELECTED BIBLIOGRAPHY

Ackerknecht, Erwin H. *A Short History of Medicine.* Baltimore: Johns Hopkins University Press, 1982.

Adkins, Lesley, and Roy A. Adkins. *Handbook to Life in Ancient Rome.* New York: Facts on File, 1994.

Bourke, John G. *Apache Medicine–Men.* New York: Dover Publications, 1993.

Estes, J. Worth. *The Medical Skills of Ancient Egypt.* New York: Science History Publications/USA, 1989.

James, Peter, and Nick Thorpe. *Ancient Inventions.* New York: Ballantine Books, 1994.

Kunow, Marianna Appel. *Maya Medicine: Traditional Healing in Yucatán.* Albuquerque: University of New Mexico Press, 2003.

Majno, Guido. *The Healing Hand: Man and Wound in the Ancient World.* Cambridge, MA: Harvard University Press, 1991.

Nunn, John F. *Ancient Egyptian Medicine.* Norman: University of Oklahoma Press, 1995.

Porter, Roy, ed. *Cambridge Illustrated History of Medicine.* Cambridge: Cambridge University Press, 1996.

Saggs, H. W. F. *Civilization before Greece and Rome.* New Haven, CT: Yale University Press, 1989.

Salzberg, Hugh W. *From Caveman to Chemist.* Washington, DC: American Chemical Society Press, 1991.

Sigerist, Henry E. *A History of Medicine. Vol. 1: Primitive and Archaic Medicine.* New York: Oxford University Press, 1987.

Starr, Chester G., ed. *A History of the Ancient World.* New York: Oxford University Press, 1991.

Sutcliff, Jenny, and Nancy Duin. *A History of Medicine.* New York: Barnes and Noble Books, 1992.

Vogel, Virgil J. *American Indian Medicine.* Norman: University of Oklahoma Press, 1970.

FURTHER READING

Billitteri, Thomas. *Alternative Medicine.* Minneapolis: Twenty-First Century Books, 2001.
   This book shows that ancient medical treatments such as acupuncture and plant remedies can be safe and effective. But the author also explores the arguments of those who oppose such treatments.

DK Publishing, *Early Humans.* New York: DK Children, 2005.
   Early humans used simple medical technology, such as plant remedies. Illustrated with full-color photos, this book examines the lives of the first peoples on Earth.

Goldsmith, Connie. *Battling Malaria: On the Front Lines against a Global Killer.* Minneapolis: Twenty-First Century Books, 2011.
   The author takes a close look at the spread of malaria around the world and what's being done to address it. The book also describes the disease, its symptoms, and treatments.

Lindsay, Judy. *The Story of Medicine: From Acupuncture to X Rays.* New York: Oxford University Press, USA, 2003.
   The author explores the history of medicine from ancient Egypt, China, India, Greece, and Rome to the present day.

Orr, Tamra. *Native American Medicine.* Broomall, PA: Mason Crest Publishers, 2003.
   This title examines how ancient Native Americans treated sickness using both medicines and magic.

Passport to History series. Minneapolis: Twenty-First Century Books, 2001-2004.
   In this series, readers will take trips back in time to ancient China, Egypt, Greece, and Rome, and to the Mayan civilization. They will learn about people's clothing, medicine, work, tools, and other aspects of daily life.

Unearthing Ancient Worlds series. Minneapolis: Twenty-First Century Books, 2008–2009.
> This series takes readers on journeys of discovery, as archaeologists discover King Tut's tomb, the royal Inca city of Machu Picchu, the ruins of Pompeii, and other archaeological treasures.

Visual Geography Series. Minneapolis: Twenty-First Century Books, 2003–2011.
> Each book in this series examines one country, with lots of information about its ancient history. The series' companion website—vgsbooks.com—offers free, downloadable material and links to sites with additional information about each country.

Whiting, Jim. *Hippocrates.* Hockessin, DE: Mitchell Lane Publishers, 2006.
> Called the Father of Medicine, Hippocrates took a scientific approach to treating illness. This book tells the story of Hippocrates and medicine in ancient Greece.

Woods, Michael, and Mary B Woods. *The History of Medicine.* Minneapolis: Lerner Publications Company, 2006.
> When treating patients, ancient healers and doctors did a lot with a little. But medical technology really took off a few hundred years ago. This book talks about the breakthroughs of modern medicine.

——. *Seven Wonders of the Ancient World.* Minneapolis: Twenty-First Century Books, 2009.
> This is one of seven books in a series that gives readers a tour of amazing monuments from throughout the ancient world. Each book focuses on the landmarks and innovations of a different region.

Zahler, Diane. *The Black Death.* Minneapolis: Twenty-First Century Books, 2009.
> This book in the Pivotal Moments in History series examines the plague that swept through Europe in the 1300s. Not only did the disease kill millions of people, it also dramatically changed European society.

WEBSITES

BROUGHT TO LIFE: EXPLORING THE HISTORY OF MEDICINE
> http://www.sciencemuseum.org.uk:80/broughttolife.aspx
> This website from the Science Museum of London presents extensive information about the history of medicine, including ancient tools, techniques, and healers.

INDIA: A SECOND OPINION
> http://www.pbs.org/frontlineworld/stories/india701/
> This website and its companion PBS television show explore ayurveda, the medicine of ancient India. The ancient practice is still alive and well in modern India.

THE MUMMY WHO WOULD BE KING
> http://www.pbs.org/wgbh/nova/mummy/
> The ancient Egyptians learned a lot about human anatomy by preparing mummies for the afterlife. This website, a companion to the *NOVA* television show of the same name, provides an introduction to mummies and mummy making.

RED GOLD: THE EPIC STORY OF BLOOD
> http://www.pbs.org/wnet/redgold/
> This website from PBS, a companion to the *Red Gold* television show, examines human blood, with historical information on bloodletting and other ancient techniques.

INDEX

ABOUT THE AUTHORS

Michael Woods is a science and medical journalist in Washington, D.C. He has won many national writing awards. Mary B. Woods is a school librarian. Their past books include the fifteen–volume Disasters Up Close series and many titles in the Seven Wonders series. The Woodses have four children. When not writing, reading, or enjoying their grandchildren, the Woodses travel to gather material for future books.

PHOTO ACKNOWLEDGMENTS